MIGRANT TO ANTARCTICA, AN ARCTIC TERN HOVERS OVER ITS ALASKA NESTING GROUND.

ALASKA'S WILDLIFE TREASURES

by Tom Melham

Prepared by the Book Division
National Geographic Society, Washington, D.C.

ALASKA'S WILDLIFE TREASURES
By Tom Melham

Published by
    The National Geographic Society
Gilbert M. Grosvenor,
    President and Chairman of the Board
Michela A. English, Senior Vice President

Prepared by The Book Division
William R. Gray, Vice President and Director
Margery G. Dunn, Charles Kogod,
    Assistant Directors

Staff for this Book
Mary Ann Harrell, Managing Editor
Thomas E. Powell III, Illustrations Editor
Jody Bolt, Art Director
Ann N. Kelsall, Penelope A. Timbers,
    Researchers
Seymour L. Fishbein, Ron Fisher,
Tom Melham, Melanie Patt-Corner,
Peter Winkler,
    Picture Legend Writers
Carl Mehler, Map Editor
Cartographic Division,
    Map Art and Production

Sandra F. Lotterman, *Editorial Assistant*
Karen Dufort Sligh,
    Illustrations Assistant
Richard S. Wain,
    Production Project Manager
Lewis R. Bassford, Timothy H. Ewing,
    Production
Karen F. Edwards, Elizabeth G. Jevons,
Peggy J. Oxford, Teresita Cóquia Sison,
    Staff Assistants

Manufacturing and Quality Management
George V. White, *Director*, John T. Dunn,

Associate Director, Vincent P. Ryan, *Manager*,
R. Gary Colbert

Bryan K. Knedler, *Indexer*

*Above: A cow moose crosses a valley rich with
summer greenery in south-central Alaska.
Pages 2-3: After a severe storm, a polar bear
shakes encumbering snow from its coat.*

ARCTIC CIRCLE

CHUKCHI

SEA

R U S S I A

Diomede
Islands

BERING

SEA

St. Lawrence
Island

YUKON DELTA

N.W.R.

Bethel ●

Nunivak
Island

*Poised on the brink of North
America, Alaska juts north from two
gently curving legs: the 1,100-mile
Aleutian chain and Southeast's
500-mile Panhandle. Two major
mountain systems rib its bulk, the
Brooks and Alaska Ranges. Between
them the Yukon River drains a vast
interior and nurtures one of the
world's largest deltas, home of
myriad birds. The Great Land
boasts extremes of size, remoteness,
and climate: from Arctic tundra to
temperate rain forest, from sea-level
wetlands to the continent's highest
peaks. Its wildlife varies
accordingly. The Bering Sea*

Pribilof
Islands

B r i s t o

B a y

A

Near
Is.

L

E

Buldir
Island

U

Rat Islands

T

I

A

N

I

S

L

A

N

D

S

*supports aggregations of marine
mammals and seabirds. Inland
regions abound with Dall sheep,
caribou, raptors, and more—
including the grizzlies and wolves
that have all but vanished from
the lower 48.*

P A C I F I C

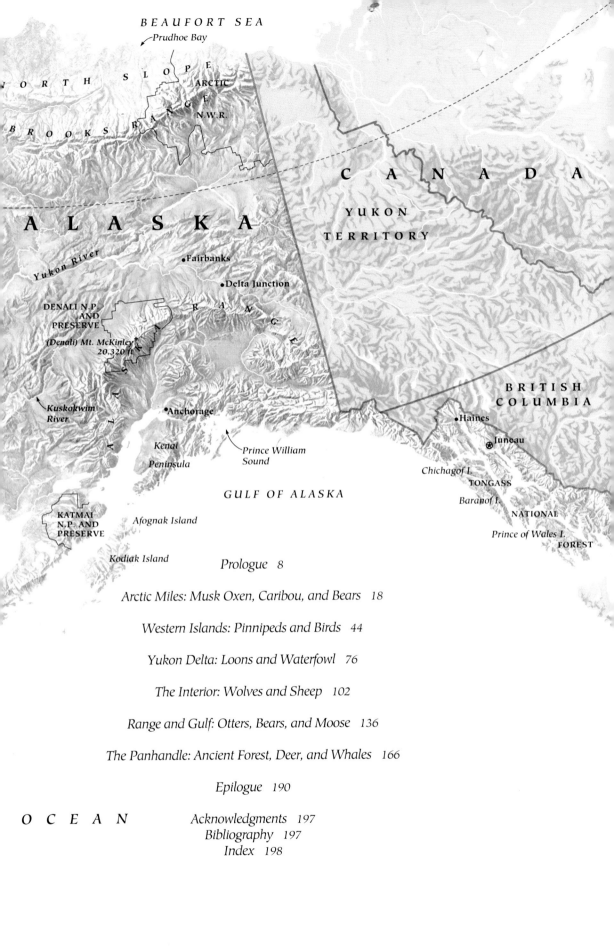

BEAUFORT SEA

Prudhoe Bay

NORTH SLOPE

ARCTIC
RANGE
N.W.R.

BROOKS RANGE

CANADA

YUKON
TERRITORY

ALASKA

Yukon River

•Fairbanks

•Delta Junction

DENALI N.P.
AND
PRESERVE

RANGE

(Denali) Mt. McKinley
20,320 ft.

ALASKA

BRITISH
COLUMBIA

Kuskokwim
River

•Anchorage

•Haines

⊛ Juneau

Kenai
Peninsula

Prince William
Sound

Chichagof I.
TONGASS

Baranof I.
GULF OF ALASKA

NATIONAL

KATMAI
N.P. AND
PRESERVE

Afognak Island

Prince of Wales I.
FOREST

Kodiak Island

OCEAN

Female caribou—deer, but always called cows—and their growing calves find abundant summer forage on a plain in Katmai National Park.

FOLLOWING PAGES: In early December, bald eagles perch in the warmth of morning sun before flying along the Chilkat River to look for food.

Prologue:
Migrants and Multitudes

Alaska beckons. Here are shallow streams choked with spawning salmon, their once silvery sides now flushed a brilliant red, their jaws so deformed they no longer close, their numberless bodies parading in a final, generational explosion of life. Here, too, brown bears shamble along shore or poise beside riffles, bulky yet incredibly agile as they routinely spear salmon in mid-leap. Bald eagles—trees full of them—ornament black cottonwood branches like Christmas decorations.

Here are islands where slumbering mobs of walrus and fur seals shingle the strands in living pavements. Clouds of raucous seabirds hang overhead like permanent smoke as murres, kittiwakes, auklets, and puffins endlessly orbit rookeries in the tens of thousands. Waterfowl and shorebirds also abound: Ragged vees of geese streak fall skies, while sandhill cranes reel past in free-form skeins that continuously ravel and unravel.

Here, caribou billow across the tundra in herds so extensive that a single band moving steadily may take hours to trot by the fixed point that is you. Hear their curious, clicking ankles—and the haunting song of the Northland's chief predator and most enduring symbol, the wolf. Here, too, gather those stolid remnants of the Pleistocene, musk oxen, whose contemporaries—woolly mammoth, short-faced bear, saber-toothed cat—long ago left this earth. They and many other species, including the continent's first humans, most likely arrived from Asia, when Siberia and Alaska were joined.

Welcome to the Great Land, the Last Frontier, that vast, elemental, and remote Serengeti-of-the-North where wildlife assumes spectacle status. Alaska is not one wildlife extravaganza, but many. Know too, however, that this richly endowed land breeds numerous wildlife myths as well: That here, every willow brake harbors a trophy moose. That even the most bumbling greenhorn has but to wet a line to secure all the salmon—or grayling or pike or trout or char—he or she could want. That deer, bear, wolf, mountain sheep, and other species abound throughout, as common here as starlings are to the lower 48. That this unspoiled northern Eden is so gigantic that man's impact here can never be great.

Such fallacies echo similar "truths" spouted by 19th-century travelers to the Great Plains. Then, bison and passenger pigeons flowed over the land; where are they now? For that matter, what has happened to so many other slices of the American pie once praised as pristine, vast, and richly endowed?

True, Alaska's web of life is gargantuan. But it is thinly spread, across a huge land wracked by climatic and seasonal extremes. Animals do not distribute themselves uniformly, not even in paradise. Walrus, for example, congregate on only a handful of Alaska's thousands of islands, while fur seals breed on just three.

Even Alaska's most abundant species are not always easily seen. Caribou, for example, move seasonally along routes that vary greatly; even experts never can be sure they will witness the animals' grand, nomadic display. Experiencing wildlife consists of being at the right place at the right time, and this is especially true in Alaska, where so many species—including whales, waterfowl, caribou, salmon, pinnipeds, and others—migrate, often spending only part of the year in the state. Others, like wolves, do not migrate but may roam great distances. Bears den up for much of the year. Some "Alaskan" species regularly range as far afield as Asia, Canada, and South America, further confounding biologists and would-be wildlife watchers. You can read pages—volumes, even—about roulette, but the game still comes down to a single spin of the wheel, and to luck. So it is with seeing Alaska's wildlife.

Alaska is, of course, a land of superlatives. More subcontinent than state, it hews to a different scale. Time slows here; space expands. Alaska boasts the nation's largest wildlife populations and its biggest wildernesses, the highest and northernmost points of mainland North America, one of the world's biggest deltas, and some of the harshest weather on earth. Almost a third of it lies within the Arctic Circle. Islands included, its total coastlines run to some 6,640 miles, more than the rest of the nation's combined. Apart from the Anchorage-Fairbanks axis and a scattering of smaller centers, Alaska remains sparsely populated even today, with only about one person for each of its 586,412 square miles of land. It is a relic, a 20th-century reminder of what most of the planet stopped being long ago: a sea of nature dotted by isolated islands of humankind. Little wonder that, to many, Alaska still epitomizes uncompromised wilderness and conjures images from Jack London's 1903 classic, *The Call of the Wild*.

And yet, sweeping changes have occurred. Alaska's human population may be less than that of the tiny District of Columbia, yet it has swelled ninefold since 1900, and small planes and snowmobiles now provide routine access to areas once considered hopelessly remote. Inevitably such changes have touched Alaska's wildlife as well as its lands.

I first visited the 49th state nearly 20 years ago, traveling by sea up the history-laden Inside Passage from Seattle. Several years later I was back, reporting on national parks that were created by the 1980 Alaska National Interest Lands Conservation Act, more commonly called the Alaska Lands Act or ANILCA. A gigantic compromise, ANILCA cobbled together the varied and often opposing interests of conservationists, developers, Native peoples, sourdoughs, state agencies, and federal bureaus. It and ANCSA—the Alaska Native Claims Settlement Act of 1971—totally redrew Alaska's map. No one group got all it asked for, but each got something. Never before had so much territory been redistributed so peacefully and grandly.

Of course, these two acts weren't fueled by idealism alone; both government and industry wanted to tap Prudhoe Bay's oil. Yet neither were they mere land-grab legislation; they embraced higher purpose. Indigenous peoples and others would be assured the right to pursue traditional lifestyles; unique wildlife and wilderness resources would be preserved for all time. Development would be wise, not wasteful. America's 19th-century mistakes in the Mid- and Wild Wests would not be repeated. The nation had been given a colossal second chance, named Alaska. That, at least, was the plan.

Returning for this book, I found that for many Alaskans, initial euphoria over ANILCA had turned to frustration. Again and again I would hear complaints of inadequacies; national parks were castigated by some as "lock-ups." Others said true wilderness was going and going fast. The state's Department of Fish and Game was managing wildlife "like a damn cattle ranch," for maximum yield of high-profile game species. Native groups, which had received huge tracts under ANCSA, were despoiling some areas and asking for more. Some of the wildest places I'd seen a few years earlier now were abuzz with small planes. And the national parks, despite huge land allotments, seemed to be suffering the same problems as Yosemite and Yellowstone—core areas were attracting too many visitors for their own good. Alaska, the ultimate outdoorsman's paradise, was getting cluttered up with people. On top of that, the same disparate groups that had benefited from ANILCA and ANCSA more than a decade earlier now wanted larger slices of the pie. But the pie hadn't grown any bigger.

In 1984, writer and environmental activist Edward Abbey passionately crystallized the emerging Northland: "Alaska is not, as the state license plate asserts, 'the Last Frontier.' Alaska is the final big bite on the American table, where there is never quite enough to go around....Alaska is where a man feels free to destroy an entire valley by placer mining, as I could see from the air over Fairbanks, in order to extract one peanut-butter jar full of gold dust....For Americans, Alaska is the last pork chop."

Size, of course, remains Alaska's most profound blessing and darkest curse. But no wilderness, not even this one, is so immense that it can survive endless dilution. A century before we plundered a seeming infinity of bison to near-extinction, Russian sealers—followed by Americans—exploited Alaska's incredibly abundant sea otters and fur seals so ruthlessly that they almost exterminated both. They and the gold-hungry sourdoughs of later times gave but two examples of how "boundless" resources prove all too finite all too soon. Greed-fueled booms and busts lie at the core of Alaskan history.

For otters and seals, human policies were reversed in time; both species came back. But Alaska's oil, timber, and commercial fishing interests often seem headed in the same old boom-and-bust direction. They tap the state's rich natural resources, often at the expense of wildlife. Clearcut logging operations routinely mar salmon streams and bear habitat in the irreplaceable old-growth forests of Alaska's southeast. As Prudhoe Bay's reserves ebb away, oilmen increasingly lobby the federal government to allow drilling in the vast Arctic National Wildlife Refuge. But ANWR is also the prime calving ground for hundreds of thousands of caribou. Overfishing the Bering Sea has seriously depleted crab and fish stocks, including what may be key species in complex food webs that have supported vast numbers of marine mammals and seabirds for ages.

Nor is industry the sole culprit. Individuals also exploit. Even some Native Americans, often idealized as environmentalists, have profiteered from land and wildlife. In 1991 visitors to remote Little Diomede Island reported that Natives were slaughtering walrus for ivory alone, while agents in a federal sting operation claimed that Natives elsewhere were trading tusks for money and drugs. Such cases are rare; far more common is the wasteful overhunting done in the name of "subsistence."

Subsistence concerns a peculiarly Alaskan right of its rural people to live off the land. Subsistence hunters can hunt otherwise-protected marine mammals, they can take waterfowl even in nesting season, and they enjoy far more generous bag limits and seasons than sport hunters do. Native Americans, of course, lived off Alaska's landscapes for numberless generations without destroying its wildlife. But today, jolting cultural changes and booming Native populations have led to excesses which have helped decrease some wildlife populations by as much as 90 percent.

Alaska's most recent boom involves ecotourism, an industry that purports to reap billions of dollars from wildlife without harming the resource. In theory, it's impeccable. Yet ecotours carry their own risky baggage; as human visitation soars, wildlife populations may suffer. Even now, cruise ships increasingly crowd key areas such as Glacier Bay, at times harassing the whales and other creatures that attract the tourists.

ANILCA established some colossal reserves—national parks, national wildlife refuges, national forests, as well as sizable private, state, and other federal entities. The nation's entire system of parks doubled in size; both wildlife refuge and wilderness acreages tripled. But numbers can mislead, and Alaska is different. Most of its national parks allow hunting, trapping, even mining. And while the federal government owns the bulk of the land here, the state manages the wildlife that lives on it. Political realities force wildlife managers to favor game species, usually through programs that control predator populations. Even on federal reserves, the wildlife web becomes more controlled by humans, less controlled by nature—and less wild.

Increasingly, we treat wildlife as a commodity, not a manifestation of undiluted nature. Subsistence and sport hunters debate who should get the larger share of each season's game "harvest." Wildlife managers are mandated to "enhance" the most "desirable" species, and talk of "maximum sustainable yields" as if Alaska's bear and moose and caribou were mere crops. Actually, they are. Even when they are not killed outright, it is man who manipulates their numbers and ranges, and all too often damages the ecosystems that sustain them, thus altering the feel of Alaska, the wild vitality that lies at the heart of this land.

Today, human visitors increasingly flock to such places as Katmai National Park and the nearby McNeil River State Game Sanctuary, to see brown bears up close. The bears quickly adapt, losing their shyness and fear of man. They aren't tame, but neither are they quite as wild as they were. As more and more humans crowd such preserves to glimpse Alaska's wild soul, they change the very things they come to see. Will this state become the world's biggest zoo?

Clearly it's not as roomy as it once was. Today's world has too many people, not enough nature, and is changing far too quickly.

This book is neither animal encyclopedia nor biological treatise. It cannot even claim to be comprehensive, though it includes material from westernmost Attu to the Canadian border, from North Slope to southeastern Panhandle. It is but one man's journey, shaped largely by encounters with wildlife biologists as I rambled the Alaskan bush during the summer of 1992. No doubt other visitors will experience vastly different situations and perspectives. They may or may not find some familiar echoes within these pages. But then Alaska beckons us all in disparate ways. So, too, does its wildlife.

FOLLOWING PAGES: Steller sea lions rest on a ledge of Chichagof Island. Their numbers have fallen despite the protection of a 1972 federal law.

FOLLOWING PAGES: BETTY SEDERQUIST / ALLSTOCK

Weatherproof winter coats give musk oxen a deceptive bulk: Long guard hairs shed rain or snow; a dense, soft undercoat preserves body heat.

FOLLOWING PAGES: Rutting caribou clash in a tangle of bared antlers. After the fall ritual the racks fall away; by summer the bulls sport velvety new ones.

ARCTIC MILES:
Musk Oxen, Caribou, and Bears

P icture—if you can—seventy or eighty thousand pregnant women, all near term. The delivery room is hundreds of miles away, on the far side of some pretty impressive mountains, and there are no ambulances, no taxis. There aren't even any roads.

Unfazed by distance or topography, the expectant mothers set off on foot, jogging through deep snow and swollen rivers, across broken Arctic terrain. No proud fathers-to-be escort them—but wolves in the mountains occasionally give chase. Amazingly, most reach their destination and give birth to healthy babies, although comforts are few and food is limited at first to leftovers—from last year. Days consist mostly of nursing the young and scrounging for snacks. Soon fresh food arrives, lots of it, but so do plague-like clouds of insects that claim more than a quart of blood a day from some victims. Yet the mothers endure, and in a few weeks pack up the kids and head for home, retracing mile after mile of their earlier trek, again on foot.

Such is the life of the caribou.

Ken Whitten grimaces. "You just can't extrapolate human experience onto caribou," he says. "They're the most efficient animals we've ever tested." A wildlife biologist with 18 years in Alaska's Department of Fish and Game, Ken adds that caribou can run up a 3,000-foot mountain, take just four or five bites of lichen at the top, and still come out ahead energywise: only a slight exaggeration. "Caribou are wanderers. They're made to move."

Good thing, because their wintering grounds and summer calving areas can be many hundreds of miles apart. Even when they're not commuting between the two, caribou mill about almost constantly, racking up perhaps twice the daily mileage amassed during migrations. They are North America's ultimate nomads.

Of Alaska's two dozen herds, the most populous inhabit the vast and gradual North Slope, which runs from the Brooks Range to the Beaufort Sea. One, the Porcupine Herd, has been Ken Whitten's specialty for more than a decade. Herds are usually named for calving areas, but this one for wintering grounds along the Porcupine River, a Yukon tributary that drains the eastern Brooks Range and northern Yukon Territory. Its members summer on the treeless coastal plain of Alaska's extreme northeast, in what man has designated the Arctic National Wildlife Refuge, or ANWR (pronounced "anwar").

Each spring they head out from the Porcupine drainage in small groups, gradually coalescing into larger and larger bands that skirt the Brooks to the east and descend the North Slope, in waves. It can be a magical time, as tens of thousands of animals simply *appear* on the bleak tundra of the refuge. Michio Hoshino, a Tokyo-based photographer who revisits ANWR every spring, still recalls his initial migration, in 1979.

"I climbed up a hill—and could see the whole North Slope. A long, long line of caribou was coming down this pass, heading north. One single line. They kept coming and coming. It was really mysterious, powerful, spectacular. Of course, I'd seen bear, moose, caribou in Denali National Park, but there had been no mystery. This time, it was as if I had seen wildlife for the first time."

To wildlife-watchers like Michio, the Porcupine Herd has become a sort of Holy Grail, steeped in mystique that stems not only from vast herd size but also from ANWR's physical remoteness and the notorious unpredictability of caribou. While the animals always return, not even biologists can predict exactly when or even where they'll arrive, since migratory routes vary tremendously. Don't expect caribou to be logical, warns Tom McCabe, a supervisory wildlife biologist with the National Biological Survey who has spent years tracking this herd.

"They'll walk right over the tops of some fairly big mountains rather than take a lower, easier route," he says. "We're not really sure why. It doesn't make sense to waste energy moving aimlessly, so they must be responding to stimuli we just don't understand."

Pregnant cow caribou arrive first on the coastal plain, dropping calves by early June. Each newborn emerges from the womb fully insulated by a high-energy layer of brown fat and a thick coat of hollow hairs that efficiently trap air. The young stand within minutes of being born, and can move fairly long distances within hours. Their mothers are drained by the journey and by the physical toll of pregnancy and lactation. Also, they are shedding old coats and growing new ones. If spring is on time, they and the calves will benefit from the tundra's highly nutritious new growth. If not, they must paw through snowpack to reach last year's remnants. Bulls and barren cows arrive later, taking advantage of browse that has had more time to green up.

Like fish that school, caribou find protection in numbers. "We call it 'predator swamping,'" says Tom. "No predators can eat everything out there. With a large group, there's also a confusion factor; you greatly reduce your individual chances of being caught." Population estimates for the Porcupine Herd, he adds, have run to 160,000 head—big, but well behind the gargantuan 420,000-member Western Arctic Herd.

"What makes the Porcupine Herd unique," says Tom, "is the fact that its aggregations are so localized, so visually stunning. We've seen groups of 120,000 or 130,000 animals, all very tightly packed, moving in a steady tide and feeding as they move. Some years, there will be cows with calves as far as you can see, bringing to mind what buffalo once looked like moving across the Great Plains, or wildebeest on the Serengeti. It's darned impressive."

Ken adds, "Sometimes you hear them before you see them. Their feet are clicking, and the cows and calves are calling to each other. You'll look up and see a continuous dark line on a hilltop, slowly spreading into a big brown smear. It moves closer, taking shape into individual caribou, shoulder to shoulder. You hear more calling, and eventually they come right by you, maybe as close as ten feet. It's not uncommon for curious young calves to run up and sniff your knees. The whole experience is overwhelming."

One reason for this herd's dramatic aggregations, he adds, is geographic. "You have 9,000-foot glaciated peaks less than 50 miles from the Arctic Ocean; all the caribou and most of the migratory birds in this part of the Slope concentrate into that narrow coastal strip. It has the reputation for being the most spectacular place to watch caribou in the world."

Hoping to glimpse the Grail myself, I head north to ANWR in late May, to a spot near the Kongakut River known, appropriately, as Caribou Pass. Tom has recommended both time and place as good bets for viewing the migration. I charter there with Fairbanks pilot Kirk Sweetsir.

In the lower 48, spring arrives as a fragrance or a singularly warm breeze. Alaska—especially *arctic* Alaska—hails spring with a shout. River ice groans and cracks, loudly. Streams roar to life, felling trees and sending them off to batter an ever wider channel through ice and gravel, to the sea.

Less than an hour out of Fairbanks, we cross the sprawling Yukon River, so oxbowed and braided that even its shore seems fluid. Breakup is well underway; huge ice chunks drift on turgid waters. Forests rise spindly and thin, attesting to brutal winters and brief growing seasons. Land rolls by endlessly, all horizontal. That is, until we reach the Brooks Range that walls off the Yukon drainage from the North Slope, dividing Alaska's interior from its far north. Rivers here still lie in winter's grasp, solid and silent. We follow one, the Kongakut, north through the mountains toward the Arctic Ocean.

Two moose, mired in deep drifts, stare up as we pass. A dozen Dall sheep stand out pure white against gray rocks. Caribou materialize: five here, ten there. As we descend the Kongakut, watery braids split from its ice-sheathed mainstream. Just before the river bursts through the northern edge of the Brooks Range and enters the coastal plain, it traces a major bend; to the east lies Caribou Pass. Game trails texture the white snow, but no animals. Good—they have not yet left the mountains. Our timing is on target.

Ice, however, blocks the gravel airstrip we had hoped to use, while blue pools of melt spatter the only other possibility—the river's icy pavement. Kirk gingerly sets the plane down on the river; slush spews from the tires, but the ice beneath holds up as he slows and taxis to within a mile of the intended airstrip. We unload my 200 pounds of gear onto the ice and, in minutes, Kirk is gone, the bray of his engine quickly fading as the plane noses south.

All about me rises a jumble of treeless, slope-shouldered hills. I am at the bottom of a fishbowl, alone, staring up at walls so bare it seems I can see everything—and everything can see me. Bright sun warms the olive drab tundra and sparkles off patches of snow. I break the 200 pounds into workable loads and start humping it the remaining mile to shore before the river ice gets any softer. Even now several braids of open water lie between me and the airstrip that is my sole ticket out of here; they can only grow larger.

Shorebound ice and rotting snow make the mainland a poor campsite, however, so I opt instead for a small gravel bar just offshore from the airstrip. By the time camp is made, the valley is socked in, first with rain, then with cold, wet snow. It could be a long five days here.

A hike east, toward Caribou Pass, takes me up a slope so gradual and bulging I feel like an ant on a beach ball. Each step reveals no new vistas, only a continuation of curving summit. Strange for a land so open to be so inscrutable; the closer I get to the saddle, the less defined it becomes. The tundra is mushy, a treacherous mix of sloppy tussocks, standing water, and decaying snow, all too wet for boots but too rugged for waders. As I near a rock outcrop, heads pop up like Indian scouts in a John Wayne movie. The caribou have arrived.

I hunker down. Ten bodies slowly emerge and ooze over the land, grazing more than migrating, taking an hour to cover a hundred yards. *These* are mothers near term, rushing to their birthing grounds? I listen to the low roar of the distant river, to chirping songbirds I never manage to see, to the incessant wind. Tiny snowflakes begin to sweep across the saddle. A curious gyrfalcon drops close and hovers like an outsize hummingbird, its speckled body stationary in the wind while wings flap rapidly, as if to shake off the wet snow. It turns, flattens, and runs with the wind, then heads upwind once more, repeating its fluttery balancing act. Then it banks a final time and streaks out of sight.

Three ground squirrels surface and dive back in their burrows, calling *sik-sik*—their Eskimo name. Hours pass as the ten caribou before me straggle downhill and ford one of the Kongakut's myriad braids. Long legs disappear in deepening waters, some animals floating the river like high-prowed, fuzzy gondolas. I look back to the summit, hoping for more, but no living flood materializes. Only snow flows through the pass. Perhaps tomorrow.

I wake to the rattle of icy rain on tent walls and peer out at the river, to check cairns I had set at water's edge. The river is up, only slightly, but enough to remind me that if I do not leave this gravel bar soon, I risk marooning myself. Moving means packing, toting, and unpacking all the gear, but then the mainland lies only a hundred feet away, just across a minor braid.

I strap on hip boots, enter the stream, and stop. Something has changed. The cairns show the braid no wider and only a bit higher than when I first arrived. But it's running much, much faster, carrying a full cargo of floating ice chunks and driftwood. Then I notice that a submerged ice platform that encased the streambed as recently as yesterday has vanished—and suddenly I realize the truth: While the river's top has barely risen, its bottom has dropped out, overnight. Breakup has rendered my cairns meaningless.

I test the crossing, find it way too deep, then try a spot where standing waves seem to promise a solid and shallower bottom. I edge in sideways, facing upstream toward the torrent of debris the river endlessly slings my way. Like a jaywalker in Manhattan, I gauge the cross-traffic and pick my way one lane at a time, slowing here and speeding there. Suddenly an icy blast rips down my right leg; the river is streaming over one boot top. It is shockingly cold, also psychologically chilling. I should have done this long ago, when it was safe. Once more I backtrack.

My next try takes me past midpoint, to within 30 feet of shore. But the water remains deep, and ice now sheathes the bottom. Currents continue to tug. I press the soft boot soles tight to the ice. Only 30 more feet.

Then the boots begin to slide, backward, faster and faster in the ongoing barrage of water, icebergs, and branches. I manage to stay on my feet, slipping and sliding like a first-time skater as I evade a riverborne tree trunk. My soles feel only ice, ice, and more ice. Then one foot senses a bare patch and grabs at it—but the other slides on. I'm in the drink. Freezing water instantly fills both waders, making them as heavy as anchors, while the overpowering current adds me to its growing collection of debris, and brushes off my puny attempts to flail closer to shore. Here I am, flat on my back, ripping along amid icebergs and downed trees on my way to the Beaufort Sea!

Instinct takes over; I roll onto my stomach and scramble spiderlike, fingernails and boot tips digging for holds but finding none. Water fills my backpack, weighing me down even more. This isn't working. I heave side-to-side, trying to roll out of the main current. There is nothing to push against but the stream of water. Heave follows heave; gradually the river slows and shallows out. Gasping, struggling, freezing, I finally stand. I've made it.

I look back to where I started—hardly a hundred yards upstream, but it seems a lifetime. Totally soaked, I dump my pack, drain what water I can from the waders without taking them off, and head downstream to find a better crossing. Now the race is on, the race against frostbite, hypothermia, and death. I find a wider and, I hope, shallower stretch and plunge through to the gravel bar. At last, a decent route! Five times back and forth I ferry the gear. Feet no longer feel. My mind is as numb as my toes.

Yet much must be done. First, set up the tent, fast. (It's windy, and you're soaked.) Don't bother with a fire. (Nice esthetics, but a waste of time.) Strip off everything above the waist and put on dry. (You can't get warm if you're wet.) Now, ditch those awful waders. (A struggle, as frozen feet cannot feel the interior lacings that trap them, and the wet rubber sticks like glue.) Frigid fingers reach in and wrestle the feet free of snarly laces. One boot off. Finally the other. Then pants and underwear. I rummage through the duffle for longjohns, jeans, and dry socks—two pairs, one for hands as well as feet—then slither into my sleeping bag and huddle in the tent, rubbing hands and feet together all the while.

Hours later, scuffling noises come from the direction of my food cache. Eyes snap open. Something is moving out there, and not just wind. Like much of Alaska, the North Slope is grizzly country, and spring is the hungriest time. I grab my rented shotgun, unzip the tent fly as quietly as possible, look out—and see nothing. Again the sound rasps: It's only a ground squirrel, rooting through a plastic bag that has fallen from the cache! A flood of relief washes over me. I put down the gun and retrieve the bag.

Leaving camp to look for caribou, I pass a patch of snow that bears a glisteningly fresh footprint, shorter than my own but half again as wide, tipped with three-inch clawmarks that remain sharply etched despite signs of melt. So, Old Bruin *was* here, not 25 yards from my tent, passing as I slept.

Just then, thrashing sounds come from the willow brake ahead. Through a thatch of branches I make out a hairy, brown hulk edged in grizzled, golden tones. It lumbers purposefully in the thicket; I cannot see the head—or even tell which end is which. Then I spot the dreaded shoulder hump. Again the shotgun comes to hand. As I follow the hump through the branches, sunlight glints off something smooth and black. Is it... horn? Yes, the massive head boss of a musk ox! Again, relief—and wonder. Strange how bearlike this leftover from the Pleistocene can appear, when expectations are up and the view is obstructed.

A second mound clears the willows. There are *two* musk oxen, both bulls, leaving the river for a gentle slope. Their hair reaches nearly to the ground, giving them the ponderous appearance of well-weathered haystacks. Yet they are light on their feet. I walk toward them openly. They see me, of course, and grow uneasy when I get within 50 yards. One trots off a bit, soon followed by the other. Then the first turns and stops, and the second runs head-on into him, horn to horn, with a deep, resounding KRAAACK. It is not defiant, nothing like the clash of rival mountain sheep, perhaps just a friendly reaffirmation of who they are.

Widespread throughout the Arctic during the Ice Ages, musk oxen vanished first from Europe and Asia, then from Alaska, as Native Americans and others hunted them out in the mid-19th century. Rifles made it easy; if unable to flee, the animals line up or circle up in a living stockade to face the threat. Only in the 1930s did musk oxen return to Alaska, imported from Greenland. A colony on Nunivak Island flourished and allowed reintroductions to other parts of the original range, including parts of the North Slope.

But where are the caribou? It is nearly June, the time when they should be assembling on the coastal plain and giving birth. I have seen perhaps twenty bands, but most contain only a few dozen animals. Where is the gypsy army, the massive, storied parade? Not in Caribou Pass, not this year. I leave for Kaktovik, a Beaufort Sea village with a Fish and Wildlife research station that is the summer base for Tom McCabe, Ken Whitten, and other biologists.

The Porcupine Herd's reputation for awesome aggregations helped fuel the creation and enlargement of ANWR, which harbors not only caribou but also what Tom calls "this great gamut of unique wildlife in a unique area"—musk oxen, eagles, grizzly bears, wolves, and millions of migratory birds that arrive from as far afield as Antarctica. The refuge's 19 million acres make it the nation's second largest wildlife reserve, after Yukon Delta. It also is one of the wildest and most remote. Lately it has been one of the more controversial as well, for it happens to lie atop what may be the nation's most promising onshore deposits of oil and natural gas.

Few wildlife refuges have been exploited for mineral development. But the Alaska Lands Act of 1980 that ceded great tracts to ANWR also included a compromise, Section 1002, which allowed that 1.5 million acres of the refuge might be opened to oil and gas drilling, pending future studies. The problem is that those 1.5 million acres—known as the 1002 or "ten-oh-two" lands—largely coincide with the Porcupine Herd's traditional calving area. So it is that, for several decades now, wildlife biologists, oilmen, wilderness enthusiasts, politicians, Native residents, and others have wrangled over ANWR's inherent imponderable: Can oil and caribou mix?

Just west of ANWR rises the Prudhoe Bay oil complex and the trans-Alaska pipeline. While it seems that ANWR's deposits do not rival Prudhoe's in size, developing them would keep both the pipeline and Prudhoe active beyond projected lifetimes. Oilmen point out Prudhoe's apparent successes: a profitable industry in a state that has seen too many boom-and-bust cycles; elevated pipelines that permit caribou to wander beneath; increases in Prudhoe's small resident herd.

Critics counter that increased hunting and human presence at Prudhoe have greatly reduced normal predator populations, causing artificial "success" for caribou. They also warn that air pollution, waste seeps, oil spills, and other environmental ills will accompany development of ANWR. Biologists add that while overhead pipes allow space for caribou, the animals often shy away from them, particularly when they're in large groups.

Pregnant cows "are especially skittish," adds Tom McCabe. "If you make any motion toward them, you're perceived as a possible predator."

Where oil exists, of course, politicians never lag far behind. It is they who ultimately will decide the fate of the 1002: oil production or wilderness. Through the Reagan and Bush years, federal and state administrations strongly favored development. The North Slope's oil money still dominates state finances, providing as much as 85 percent of Alaska's annual revenues. It also bankrolls the vast, Native-run North Slope Borough and pays every state resident a yearly "dividend" of about a thousand dollars. Even dedicated wilderness activists have despaired that drilling in ANWR was only a matter of when, not if. But in 1989, *Exxon Valdez* ran aground in Prince William Sound. By producing the nation's worst oil spill, it also granted ANWR's wilderness a reprieve.

Today, politicians cannot ignore ANWR's wildlife resources. Many seek advice from biologists like Ken Whitten and Tom McCabe, who heads research programs for the 1002. Just how important is this area to caribou? How might they react to concentrated human activity? Could they calve someplace else?

Ken answers: "There's little argument among professional biologists—even those in the oil industry—that this area is important, long-term, for calving. Work we've done over the past ten years indicates there's higher survival when calving occurs in the 1002 area than when it occurs elsewhere."

One good reason, he thinks, is the coastal plain's scarcity of predators. Wolves and grizzly bears keep more to the foothills of the Brooks Range, where terrain and cover favor successful hunts. The plain's wide-open tundra, in contrast, enables caribou to spot danger in time to outrun it. Yet another advantage of the coastal plain, Tom McCabe believes, is its excellent forage, nutritionally some of the best in the herd's entire range—once the summer sun works its wonders. Sprawling, low-profile tundra may seem visually uniform, but, says Tom, "It's one of the most diverse plant communities I've seen. There's a tremendous number of microhabitats. It's like a three-tiered rain forest that's ankle deep."

Different plants put forth at different times, spawning a continuous feast of top-quality fodder that is vital to the caribou, which also are in a race. Females must nurse calves, replenish lost reserves, put forth winter coats and new antlers. Bulls also need to gear up for cold weather and for the fall rut, when they duel for the right to sow the seeds of the next generation.

For several years now, biologists have sought to learn precisely how the coastal plain serves the Porcupine Herd's nutritional needs. Because of the huge numbers and vast spaces involved, they rely heavily on radio collars, which help them track specific animals over weeks and even months. To collar caribou, of course, you first must catch them. Dart guns or nets bring down adult animals; for calves, however, it's more of a cowboy operation, by helicopter.

"Off to the roundup," says Tom as the chopper carrying him and others rises and veers across the tundra, all eyes scanning for caribou. Soon he targets a particular calf. The pilot touches down; two biologists burst out and give chase across the boggy tundra. It is cold, wet, exhausting work, sprinkled with open-field tackles made and missed. Once down, the bleating youngster is weighed, measured, sexed, fitted with an expandable radio collar, and released—all within 70 seconds.

Usually the calf's mother stays near, despite scurrying humans and deafening rotors, trotting nervously this way and that, watching, occasionally calling out in a motherly bray. The calf answers with a burp-like croak. Set free, it dutifully bounds off to momma, who greets it with licks and sniffs of recognition, and the pair wanders slowly away as if nothing had happened.

But sometimes the mother vanishes, or the calf bolts in the wrong direction. Every moment apart increases the chance that a golden eagle or wolverine might move in. The collaring operation, Tom concedes, puts some animals at risk, but he sees no practical alternative.

"The range of this herd," he says, "is an area the size of Montana. As biologists, we'd just as soon not have to disturb these animals at all. But it's like anything else—you have to sacrifice something to gain something."

Once collars are in place and the caribou-wrangling is over, airborne trackers daily relocate each collared animal by monitoring its radio signal. They note the vegetation around it to see which plant communities draw most caribou. Several times during the summer, researchers also recapture and reweigh collared calves, to link weight gains to particular habitats.

I am in a spotter plane over the Beaufort Sea, which today resembles nothing so much as an Escher print: Blocky patches of snow alternate with blue splotches of bare sea ice as far north as the eye can see. Pilot Roger Kaye and biologist Don Young are seeking collared calves. We head for the semifrozen sponge of tundra, tawny and endlessly textured with bogs, ponds, spaghetti-like streams, and the irregular polygons born of repeated freeze-and-thaw cycles. The coastal plain is stark, unspoiled, almost eerily empty.

Antennas sprout from each wing strut of the Cessna, enabling Roger to determine the direction of incoming radio signals. Don hunches over a receiver; since each collar transmits at a different frequency, he can tell which calf is which. We all wear headsets, to monitor the incoming bleeps.

"Let's take this one," says Don, and Roger banks to the right.

Dead ahead, a caribou clump scatters. Don spots the collared animal, notes our position, and then listens for another signal. He finds one, but it's weak. Roger lifts a wing to the sky and circles, to enhance the antenna's directionality. Steadily he homes in on the ever stronger bleep, and soon Don has another visual.

So it goes, over and over, as they wade through a list of frequencies and plot each calf's location. The count swells to 56, only two short of the total functioning, and by now we're in the foothills of the Brooks Range.

The coastal plain is not an Eden, not even for caribou. The snowmelt that speeds plants into vitality also pools atop the permafrost, giving rise to insect hordes that make life nearly unbearable. Ken Whitten elaborates: "There's a botfly that squirts larvae into the caribou's nose, where they take hold. Warble flies lay eggs on the caribou's back or legs, and the larvae hatch out and burrow under the skin. But mosquitoes are by far the dominant insect pest. In the first part of July, they come out in droves."

Adds Tom, "That's when the caribou all smash together on the coastal plain and you see tremendous, tight-knit aggregations of tens of thousands of animals, virtually shoulder to shoulder. Like they're in a corral."

Consider it a form of predator swamping, with caribou aggregating most closely on calm days, when no winds deter the pests. Often they mill about, or head for the coast in search of a breeze. They seem less wary, almost nearsighted. Stand quietly before an oncoming mass of caribou on such a day and they just keep coming, momentarily parting around you and rejoining immediately afterward, like the biblical waters of the Red Sea.

The insects, Tom adds, are not *all* bad, and in fact constitute an essential part of the ecosystem. "A lot of shore birds come to the tundra specifically because there's lots of insects, lots of food here." Even caribou may benefit indirectly from the bugs, since the pests keep them moving and thus help prevent overgrazing the harsh yet delicate coastal plain. Because of insect harassment, he says, caribou stay only about six weeks. "Generally by mid-July they're gone—they start moving south. The uplands tend to be breezier, cooler, drier, with less breeding opportunity for insects."

Also by then, forage on those higher elevations is at its best. The fall migration ensues, as caribou take what Tom describes as "a sort of Genghis Khan approach. You get all 200,000 animals moving along together. It's called an alimental migration—they're moving to their food resource." Hence the caribou as perpetual motion machine. To live off this land forever, you have to keep moving.

I spend part of my last day on the refuge with pilot Dennis Miller, who flies his own SuperCub for wildlife researchers. The Cub is to the Cessna as a sports car is to a station wagon: lighter, more maneuverable, parkable almost anywhere. Its fabric fuselage, barebones cockpit, and flaplike doors make it seem less a plane and more a kite with wings.

Potholes, polygons, and dark, wriggly wisps—caribou tracks—maze the tundra. No animals, however. You'd think 200,000 caribou would be easy to spot on the tablelike coastal plain, but it's just too huge. Off to starboard, the Brooks Range gleams starkly white. It and the tundra enchant you; that such a vast and wild place remains anywhere today is a statement in itself. Dennis spots a few animals and turns inland. Suddenly the tundra writhes with life, as if infested by maggots. A roiling mass of caribou, loosely spread over two or three miles, oozes toward us and the coast: the mother lode! Most animals, appropriately, are cows. They grow increasingly dense, impossible to count or even estimate. Do 10,000 or 50,000 trot atop the saddle ahead? Make your wildest guess and double it, the biologists say, and still it will be too low.

Dennis swings back, following the animals now, estimating that 90 or 95 percent of the herd trots beneath our wings. He overtakes the vanguard and scans for landing sites, then touches down on a dry wash. We walk to the highest ground around—the bank of the wash—and wait for the animals to come to us. Soon they approach, staring at us and sniffing the wind cautiously, but not stopping. They seem both preoccupied and curious. One group engulfs the Cub in a living tide. Beyond, loose bunches of animals parade across the land as far as we can see. We are in their very midst, and visions of Indians at the Little Bighorn whistle through my mind. The wind whistles too—it's picked up so much that I can no longer hear the grunts or clicking hooves. The caribou move nimbly but without haste, grazing as they play their gigantic game of follow-the-leader. Hundreds pass; thousands more emerge from the horizon to replace them. *Everything* moves. I look away, to an empty spot of tundra and *it* seems to move, as eye and brain struggle to make sense of a landscape in nonstop motion.

We watch for about an hour, spellbound. By chance, the advance legions turn back toward us. They and the still-advancing army converge like waves on a beach, sliding by here, merging there. The march becomes a diaspora.

Still the wind builds, to 25 knots or so; this is the caribou's realm, not mine. The bleating calves, the burps and calls of cows, the clickety-clacks of their feet all chorus: We exist. Yet it is ephemeral music, for in a few more weeks they will be off, steadily dispersing as they wend toward the winter range. Summer's brief crescendo of life will have faded for this year, as the mobs melt back into the wild vastness of the Arctic. Now you see them, now you don't.

How might oil drilling impact this timeless scene? One scientist believes "it's naive to think we could build anything the size of Prudhoe Bay and *not* have an effect on wildlife." He adds that the amount of oil may not justify the risks. "The average guesstimate here is 3.2 billion barrels. Prudhoe initially had some ten billion barrels. Even if we had a field like Prudhoe working by A.D. 2000, we would not reduce our need for imports by much—maybe 5 percent. We'd *still* be getting something like 65 percent of our oil from overseas. By no stretch of the imagination is there enough oil in ANWR to make any significant difference in the U.S. dependence on foreign oil." In other words, all ANWR's oil, delivered now, would keep America's cars on the road only a few months. Then it would be gone, and the coastal plain would be changed, permanently.

Caribou-watcher Michio Hoshino observes, "Oil people say what they do won't affect caribou—it may be true. Nobody knows. Government in Alaska says that caribou are so far away that 99 percent of the people—even in Alaska—never see a caribou migration in their lives. But that's OK. The importance is that it exists, still. Just like with wolves—you don't have to see a wolf, but it's a very good feeling to know that somewhere in this world wolves still live."

He adds, "I think there are two forms of nature. One is the nature you see every day. The other aspect of nature is something very distant, very remote. You don't see it, but you know it's there. It's spiritual. It has to do with imagination, with soul. Without this kind of nature, our daily life may not change, but something—soul—is missing. To me, caribou are like that."

The caribou, meanwhile, were pulsing south, to the foothills and beyond, following the Arctic's timeless rhythms.

FOLLOWING PAGES: Caribou cross the braided valley of the Kongakut River, roaming on the coastal plain near the Brooks Range foothills.

FOLLOWING PAGES: MICHIO HOSHINO

STEPHEN J. KRASEMANN / DRK PHOTO   GARY SCHULTZ

VERNA E. PRATT / ALASKAKRAFTS, INC.   FRANK G. PRATT / ALASKAKRAFTS, INC.

*O*nly days old, a caribou calf stays with its mother on the coastal plain north of the Brooks Range, in Arctic National Wildlife Refuge (ANWR). Epic wanderers, Porcupine Herd caribou arrive here in spring to calve and browse on emerging tundra plants. Arctic willow (above left) provides occasional nibbles. Caribou rely heavily on tender young shoots of tussock cottongrass, not the namesake blossoms (far left); they relish the woolly lousewort (left), a wildflower that blooms from late May into mid-June.

JOHNNY JOHNSON (BELOW); LOWELL GEORGIA (OPPOSITE)

*E*ggs over—lightly. Around midnight of a midsummer day, when the sun never sets, a yellow-billed loon somewhere in ANWR turns the incubating eggs. Should the waterside nursery succeed, the clutch of three will make a welcome addition to the rarest of the five loon species. Yellowbills number perhaps 4,000 in Alaska, 15,000 worldwide. Autumn rusts the marshy coastal tundra (opposite), and winter freezes it. By then, the yellowbills have departed to open fishing grounds. Some were wintering on Prince William Sound when oil from the Exxon Valdez fouled it in 1989.

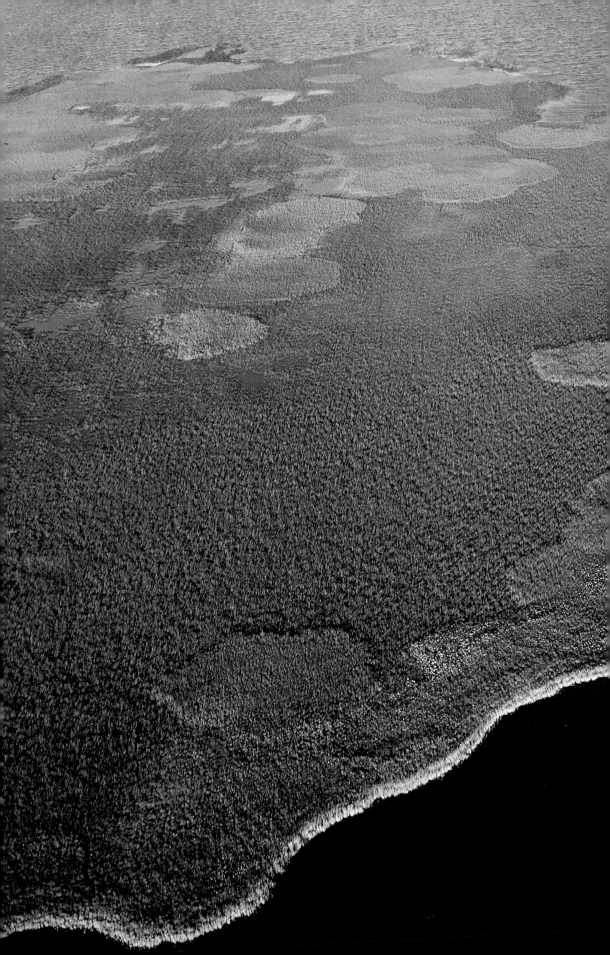

White hunter of polar seas and subarctic estuaries, the beluga whale haunts the shallows for fishes, squid, crabs, and worms. Its name derives

from the Russian byelukha—*white whale. The varied distinctive sounds it makes, including trills and chirps, inspired its vernacular name "sea canary."*

*T*he quick white fox pounces on a vole, which
the bushy-tailed hunter has heard stirring
beneath the North Slope snow. Only in
summer does the Arctic fox wear the brownish
gray standard farther south. Another form of
the species wears brown, charcoal, or blue-
gray fur. Lemmings, such as the doomed
captive below, often provide a diet mainstay;
when lemmings crash, fox pups may starve.
Raider and scavenger as well as hunter, the
Arctic fox rifles seabird rookeries, feasts on
stranded whales, roams the pack ice for tidbits
of seal left by polar bears. It also hangs out at
settlements, where friendly humans risk rabies
by offering handouts.

FOLLOWING PAGES: Polar bears in Alaska—
like this playfully sparring pair from Hudson
Bay—often prowl the pack ice in search of
ringed seals, a favorite prey. Adult males
usually hunt alone; cubs stay with their
mother about 28 months.

STEPHEN J. KRASEMANN / DRK PHOTO (ABOVE); GARY SCHULTZ (OPPOSITE)
FOLLOWING PAGES: STEPHEN J. KRASEMANN / PETER ARNOLD, INC.

LON E. LAUBER; FOLLOWING PAGES: STEVEN C. WILSON / ENTHEOS

Why fight? Flaunting their tusks, rival walrus may end an imbroglio without a blow. Bigger pair wins. If it's too close to call, the ivories dig in.

FOLLOWING PAGES: A squawk ruffles feathers of Unalga Island nesters. The cormorant rears; the gull swoops; and the Aleutian sky, as ever, threatens.

WESTERN ISLANDS:
Pinnipeds and Birds

The voice was cheery, booming over the outboard's guttering rumble; the words, however, bordered on the ominous. "Islands out here don't have a leeward side. They're all shaped like footballs—no place to hide when the seas come up." Don Winkelman, the speaker and charterboat captain, steered his 28-foot cruiser from Togiak into Bristol Bay, off southwestern Alaska. He was taking me and three others 35 nautical miles out, to tiny Round Island, one of seven isles that make up Walrus Islands State Game Sanctuary.

Like Alaska's more distant western isles, Round Island offers a distinctive wildlife experience. Also like them, it is small, remote, expensive to get to, and exposed to the vagaries of the notorious North Pacific. It lies close in, but access is limited by law as well as by weather: no more than 12 campers, every five days.

We set out amid reports of three-foot seas and winds blowing 15 to 20 miles an hour. In the minutes it took to clear the harbor channel, they'd increased to six feet and a solid 20. Don cut back to seven knots, then to four—about a sixth of his usual speed. The boat laboriously climbed each wave to the crest, then dropped down the back. Soon the seas doubled again, to the twelve-foot range; the boat bottomed hard into every trough, each time slam-dunking my backbone into the stiff bench seat.

Yes, I'm a landsman. Staring out from a roller coaster at an endless procession of waves, at islands that never grow near, gets old to me very fast. Don, ever smiling, explained the area's peculiarities: The shallow bottom off Togiak magnifies tidal effects, the offshore islands create some weird currents, and the wind often blows in your face. Today all three factors were against us. Once, he'd made Round Island in only 47 minutes; today, five hours of wallow-and-slam would drag by before we finally stood off our goal.

True to his warning, Round Island had no real harbor; its Boat Cove was but a shallow dimple in a rocky and barnacled coast. A tiny Zodiac inflatable nudged toward us from shore, as we rocked in the chop. One at a time we jumped from Don's aluminum bronco to the madly pitching Zodiac; it was a bit like getting off a bus while it's moving through world-class potholes. Near shore we reversed the drill, leaping off the bouncing raft and grabbing at crags and outstretched hands. Only then did I notice several walrus nearby, gray as the rugged shingle they slumbered upon, apparently unconcerned.

Since the state set up the sanctuary in 1960, Round Island has been closed to all hunting. A permit system so tightly limits day and overnight visitation that this island is more protected than any national park. An unusual situation, given that it is managed by Alaska's Department of Fish and Game, which primarily regulates sport hunting and fishing, and espouses a policy of "maximum use." Even the name—"game sanctuary" rather than "wildlife sanctuary"—points up departmental priorities. Legally the state *cannot* manage marine mammals because they, like seabirds, are under federal regulation. Yet seabirds and walrus are Round Island's main residents. So, although the general rule in Alaska is that the feds own the land and the state manages the wildlife, here the reverse is true. Except that the state effectively controls hunting by limiting access. Round Island is a strange place.

Polly Hessing, one of Round Island's two live-in wildlife technicians, told me that before it became a sanctuary, "fishermen used to come to the island when they wanted a break. They were all over the place. They would drive their boats up to the beach, the walrus would all go in the water and bob around. It was fun and picturesque for everybody—except for the walrus." Now, she added, small boats must keep to a three-mile limit, while bottom-dragging trawlers give the island a 12-mile berth. Such rules and the hunting ban have led to bad feelings in some coastal villages, but Polly carefully explains the department's position.

"There are six other islands in the sanctuary, but this is the only one with restricted access. It's the one place in North America the natives can't hunt walrus. They can hunt them anywhere else, whenever they want."

Indeed, walrus also congregate on the nearby Twin Islands and on several mainland sites around Bristol Bay. But local Yupik Eskimos maintain that they traditionally hunted here—and in fact sometimes do in the fall, after sanctuary staff leave the island but before all the animals do. They want the state to give formal sanction to a hunt. Sanctuary wildlife biologist Larry Van Daele summed up the situation as "a conflict of cultures. Our culture says if you *protect* something, that's the best way to let it live in perpetuity. The Yupik culture says, if you *don't* use something, it's going to go away."

About a mile wide by two miles long, Round Island rises to a lone 1,400-foot summit that gives it the profile of a single-masted sailboat. It is absolutely treeless; not a shrub, not a living stick stands anywhere. Yet except for its rocky shore and steepest cliffs, it is green as Ireland, thanks to a persistent wrapping of cloud and fog and mist. During my five-day stay, rain fell for four and a half. Tents and gear soaked on the voyage over never dried out. But the myriad wildflowers, grasses, and sedges grew incredibly lush.

On the north end, winds gusted hard enough to blow me off-trail at times, yet the fog refused to lift. Near the top of a rise, I got a whiff of something, something bad. A few steps farther, black-legged kittiwakes materialized from the mist, cluttering every niche and crevice and garden apartment in a natural highrise that dropped sheer to the sea. I'd entered a rookery. Squat murres—white-breasted, black of head and back—stood and stared. Tall, dark cormorants spaced themselves like sentries on a blocky parapet.

Then there were puffins—both tufted and horned. To my eye, these colorful seabirds wear their wings too far aft to support their chunky bodies adequately. Definitely not svelte soarers, they flap furiously, expending what seems inordinate effort to go from cliff to sea and back again. But they get around just fine. They do especially well underwater, where, like penguins, they "fly" through the ocean in pursuit of fish.

Beyond the rookery, the island curved out in a scimitar coast where about a thousand walrus basked—if, indeed, any animal can be said to "bask" in a 20- or 30-knot rainstorm, atop bare and frigid rock. They were pinker than the Boat Cove animals, indicating they were warmer and had been out of water longer. Here and there, algae from the rocks had tinged their warty, tuberculed skin with green. Some backs and hindquarters were visibly bloodied from sparring. A terrific stench—similar to that of a pungent cheese, well aged—permeated the air.

In summertime, Round Island becomes one huge stag beach party:

Two-ton male walrus sporadically come ashore to joust and bellow and snooze and have a roaring good time. Walrus cows shun the place, preferring to summer with calves and yearlings far to the north, in the pack ice of the Chukchi Sea. Dr. Francis H. (Bud) Fay, a University of Alaska professor who has spent the better part of a lifetime studying this species, notes that sexual segregation lets both sexes concentrate on their main summer activities: feeding and resting. Males haul out on Round Island for two or three days between week-long bouts of serious feeding throughout Bristol Bay. They may seem boorish and sleepy on land. But at sea they dive almost continually, foraging for bottom-dwelling clams and snails. They can't open the shells, but they take a mollusk into their mouths and chew off any protruding morsels. Strange for such clumsy-looking fellows—1,600 pounds for a small bull—to feed on such diminutive prey. Stranger still, they ingest huge amounts of gravel and stones for reasons not fully understood.

Some days, Round Island's beaches hold only a few dozen walrus, yet the animals always pack tightly together, often in tiers with heads in the same direction. Though nearby stretches of shingle lie empty, new arrivals inevitably head straight for the mob. As I watch, one big, light-colored bull wallows ashore and takes aim on the congregation's very core. Ponderously he forces a way over and through his blubbery buddies, sparking screams of protest and minor jousting: Tusks clack, maws roar, heads jab. The monster male literally rolls over the opposition's initial ranks, then pauses, as if he forgot where he was going—or decided it wasn't worth the effort—and drops with a thud I can feel. He looks dead asleep.

All around him, fore and hind flippers occasionally stretch forth from lozenge-like bodies. They are massive and stubby, yet surprisingly dexterous, unfolding like those long, delicate fans favored by Victorian ladies. One pats a companion's beefy shoulder, then turns and gently strokes its owner's anatomy. Large, flat toenails gleam like dark, embedded jewels.

A few minutes later the narcoleptic intruder rises and lumbers farther inland, savagely poking and bulling his way while others respond with the usual walrus goodwill—more grumbling and tusk jabbing. He beats up a smaller walrus until it becomes a sort of escort, softening up resistance ahead like an icebreaker preceding a battleship. Then abruptly the big bull stops, reels heavily to one side, rams his massive head into a neighbor—and goes to sleep. A blissful, gurgling sigh escapes his bristly lips, not unlike the sound my bathtub makes as the last water drains out. Ahh. Home at last.

Why all the jousting, I wonder, if the purpose in coming here is to rest? Walrus beach life didn't seem very tranquil to me. Bud Fay explains: "It's considerably more restful than their winter behavior, when adult males are essentially solitary. Then, when they do meet, they fight. Fights can be very intense, with lots of action and usually a lot of blood."

Late one night I wake to walrus growls and splashings and some extended *brrrawwwrrrrs* that sound like three-year-olds bubbling into their milk. Rain is falling in a dead calm. I hear clicks off to the left, low-pitched, primeval grumblings to the right. The usual wheezings and gargles of daytime also occur, accompanied now and then by brief, reedy whistles that have shrill edges yet seem almost whispered.

More belches from across Boat Cove, a tympani chorus. And then I hear what the experts all have talked about but I've not experienced until now: the resonant, chime-like "gonging" of the walrus. It's in the human mid-range, loud and rich, a percussive *"ping, ping, pong, ping"* that resembles the sound of plucked strings. Pitch and sequence vary, bunching the "pings" into out-of-tune chords whose disharmony only adds to their resonance and eerie nature. Amid background wails and tympani, amid clicks and piccolo-like whistling, amid the snores, grunts, burblings, and all other vocal outpourings of the walrus repertoire, gonging could be a bell for the dead. I found it as enchanting, addictive, and baffling as the songs of humpback whales.

In fact, this summertime serenade is but a jam session performed mostly by younger males. Says Bud with a chuckle, "The older ones have been doing it all winter, and they're tired of it. The sounds youngsters make at Round Island have all the right elements but they're mixed up in order. Or they only have a few elements down, rather than all. They don't get it right, apparently, until they're big enough to breed."

Come autumn and the approach of the breeding season, he adds, bulls head north to search for females. "When the females haul out on the ice, males take up positions along the edge and go through this repetitive display of whistling and chattering their teeth—or however they make the clicks—and gonging. If you find a male doing that and you put a hydrophone in the water, you hear dozens of others in the area doing exactly the same thing. In exactly the same order. Underwater. We're not sure whether this is to attract females or simply to let other males know they're there and warn them not to try to horn in."

The morning after the Boat Cove concert, Don Winkelman arrives with more visitors. He approaches slowly, killing the engine, and Polly begins ferrying people ashore in the Zodiac. Suddenly, without apparent reason, the animals stampede. Gigantic, clumsy bodies tumble every which way in a frantic rush to the sea, crashing atop one another, with some heads wedging among rocks for a moment or two. I see a tusk break, hear groans and thuds of flesh on flesh, all around. Seconds later, the cove is a roiling mass of bodies and froth. Polly, deeply upset, sits and shakes her head. I recall an earlier conversation with her: "We're juggling goals of visitation and public education versus trying to protect walrus from harassment. It's difficult, because as long as you have people coming to a place like this, you lose something. That's the trade-off. I don't want to pretend—'Oh, it's a sanctuary, come one, come all'—I want recognition that there's a cost involved."

Despite crusty exteriors, walrus are sensitive to environmental change and hunting pressure. Russians—and, later, Americans—so valued walrus ivory that in places like the Pribilof Islands they "essentially exterminated" the animals, says Bud Fay. "Throughout Alaska, walrus were depressed rather severely from the mid-1800s through to the 1950s. Then they were given some protection and allowed to increase, to what we now suppose is something like their original numbers, somewhere around 250,000."

Even so, they have not returned to the Pribilofs, 350 miles west of Round Island. Fur seals—also nearly hunted out and later allowed to recover—took over former walrus haulouts there. In size—especially given Alaska's grandiose scale—the Pribilofs are microscopic, volcanic dots in the middle of the Bering Sea. Biologically, however, they harbor one of the largest and most dramatic collections of wildlife anywhere on the continent, because they lie at the outer edge of the highly productive continental shelf. Half a dozen varieties of marine mammals and more than a hundred species of seabirds come here seasonally to breed and rear young. The island of St. George, for example, boasts a million murres and perhaps 200,000 red-legged kittiwakes—95 percent of the world population.

Humans were latecomers to the Pribilofs, first arriving in 1786, when Russian voyager Gerassim Pribilov discovered here what other sealers had sought unsuccessfully for decades: the mother lode. About three-fourths of the world's northern fur seals breed here, in summer. The rest of the year they scatter along the North Pacific rim, from the Kuriles north of Japan to southern California. Until Pribilov's discovery, sealers had to hunt the animals at sea in small groups; now they could harvest them wholesale.

Here also were walrus, Steller sea lions, and sea otters. A Russian trading company quickly moved to exploit the Pribilofs' "soft gold" by enslaving Aleut hunters and moving them from their Aleutian Islands homeland, to harvest animals and prepare hides. In the process, the Russians introduced European diseases and alcohol; American traders followed suit after 1867; neither Aleuts nor seals prospered.

Both, however, survived. Today, about 600 descendants of sealers, settlers, and Aleuts inhabit these islands. Most bear Russian surnames, and the town church remains Russian Orthodox. About a million fur seals converge here in summer, occupying two sorts of sites: haulouts, resting spots used by males that have not won mates, and rookeries, where each successful bull surrounds himself with a harem of as many as a hundred breeding females, plus newborn pups. I visited one rookery with George (Bud) Antonelis, a biologist with the National Marine Fisheries Service, which oversees marine mammal research and plays a role in regulating commercial fishing.

The rookery, known as Reef, literally crawled with life. Tens of thousands of seals packed themselves onto a quarter-mile strip of basalt beach; acrid smells and constant caterwauling filled the air. Big, dark, mustachioed beachmasters—mature bulls, each weighing 500 or 600 pounds—studded the beach every 20 or 30 feet, erect and watchful, each reigning over a territory whose borders were invisible to all but them. Females, only a fifth as big as the males, came and left at will. Clumped helter-skelter by the score were tiny, sleek, black pups, only a week or so old, napping or suckling or squalling for mothers off in the surf.

Beachmasters, ponderous from a winter of constant feeding, lead fascinatingly schizophrenic lives. From late August through October, males leave the island to become creatures of the sea, roaming alone, rarely touching land until they begin returning in May. But in summer they mass on the Pribilofs, totally shunning the ocean and waging frightening, often bloody turf wars as they select and fiercely defend individual territories. By late June, females begin showing up; the bulls call, wooing them near while they remain in place lest rivals usurp their hard-won fiefdoms. As females approach, the romance-driven bulls do all they can to hold them. The females, however, have other priorities.

To begin with, most are pregnant, from the previous summer's mating, and are coming ashore to deliver their ten- to fourteen-pound pups. They do so within a day or two; four to six weeks later they are in estrus, ready to mate again, and the males oblige. Unlike bulls, females freely return to the sea to feed, and soon embark on a cycle of nursing pups for a few days, then feeding for about a week at a time. Pups sprawl among the bulls, who can do little to provide for them and are preoccupied with gathering more females. At times, the young stray into different territories. Bulls ignore these minor incursions, and also tolerate the females' continual comings and goings. But should a mature male—or, for that matter, a human—intrude, they are on it in a flash. Make no mistake: These recumbent fat guys in sleek sealskin coats pack three-inch canines. They are *predators*. Bud told of two biologists who fell into a rookery when the cliff they were on suddenly collapsed.

"One was knocked unconscious by the fall. The other tried to get out and was just torn apart by the males, bit so many times that he bled to death. The first one just lay there in a hump. The only reason he survived was he looked like a lifeless mass, just another rock on the beach."

Nevertheless, Bud says *we* will venture into the very midst of Reef today. An observational catwalk makes this possible. It's a bit ramshackle, a continuous scaffold-on-stilts about seven feet high that staggers through the rookery like a derelict pier from some long-abandoned port. While it's not much to look at, it constitutes a marvelous bit of sleight-of-hand. Walk on the beach and we would be ripped to bits. But crawl atop the catwalk, and the animals hardly react—though they clearly see us just a few feet above their noses. Pups slumber, females nurse and yowl for offspring, bulls glare at each other but not at us. Apparently, their territories are only two-dimensional. By coming in from above, we enter their world without challenging them, almost as if we are invisible men.

Oh, to be a bull fur seal, surrounded by a harem of 40 or 50 or even 100 willing females. What a sybarite! That, at least, is a popular notion. But consider that beachmasters remain landbound for two arduous months, within sight of water but unable to take even a brief dip for fear their territory and harem will be taken by another. Their self-imposed exile means a summer-long fast. Yet they must remain ever alert, fending off intruders, attracting and satisfying the female mobs that come and go, to say nothing of putting up with countless pups underfoot—all without so much as an anchovy or a beer. Sybaritic life, indeed! No wonder that they rarely live beyond their early teens, while females survive and breed even into their 20s. No wonder beachmasters are so grumpy.

Females, actually, are the freest spirits of the fur seal world.

"The young are pretty much left on their own," says Bud. "There's no indication that females teach pups how to swim or even take them to the water. Even when they migrate in fall, mothers don't travel south with the pups; they leave independently." Of the new generation, a majority—somewhere between 50 and 90 percent—will not see their second birthday. Why don't mothers show more maternal care? Bud answers that, like many aspects of seal behavior, "it's still a mystery."

A major problem of seal research, he adds, is that the subjects spend most of their lives at sea, where they can't be observed easily. Tracking them across the vast North Pacific by ship or small plane is technically but not economically possible; it just isn't feasible. Even if it were, researchers couldn't observe what the animals do underwater. But now, a breakthrough: satellite "tags." These space-age versions of radio collars, Bud explains, come equipped with saltwater switches, pressure transducers, and other electronic wizardry that enable them to gauge water temperature and depth, dive time, location, and other particulars. They store such information, beaming it to scientists via communications satellites whenever the animal surfaces. No planes or boats are needed.

"Until now," he says, "the behavior and movements of fur seals at sea have been a void. With satellite technology, we're on the verge of detailing exactly where animals are going, what they're eating, and how they're foraging when they get there." Like radio collars, however, the new rigs are limited; batteries last only two or three months, and each unit costs about $3,500. Still, Bud and others hope the devices will help determine, among other things, why fur seal populations on nearby St. George Island "have been declining the last ten, fifteen years, at about 6 percent a year."

Of even greater concern is the precipitous drop, since 1960, in Steller sea lions. These are stately creatures twice the size of northern fur seals, with lighter, tawny coats. Thomas Loughlin, a NMFS wildlife biologist, heads the Alaska Ecosystems Program and is "in charge of all the government's marine mammal work that takes place in Alaska outside of the ice." In 1992, he estimated the worldwide population of the Steller at "about 100,000 and declining, a third of what there were in the '60s and early '70s. We don't know why." While this species, unlike fur seals, breeds throughout its North Pacific range, its Pribilof population has been especially hard hit.

"There used to be 3,000 pups born here every year," said Tom. "Now it's down to a few hundred. We know what it's not; we don't know what it is. It's not redistribution. It's not pollutants or contaminants. It's not increased predation. But there's still a lot of other things out there it could be." He anticipates another five or six years of research to determine the causes.

Pribilof Islander Larry Merculieff, city manager of St. Paul, feels he and other Pribilovians have had the answer for decades, while a bureaucracy dominated by commercial fishing interests has consistently failed to see the light. The National Marine Fisheries Service, after all, is part of the U. S. Department of Commerce, where economic priorities tend to outweigh biological ones. The cause of sea lion and seal declines, he says, is obvious: overfishing of the once fecund Bering Sea.

The Bering—shallow, cold, and nutrient-rich—has gained in importance as other major fisheries have been fished out. Its major catch is not the celebrated king crab or salmon, but a creature few Americans recognize in the raw: a bottom-feeding groundfish known as walleye pollock. It is ugly, its flesh bland but useful; most of it winds up as *surimi,* a paste that emerges in supermarket coolers as imitation crab and lobster, or as fish cakes.

In 1991, a record five million metric tons of pollock were harvested, the largest single-species catch in the world. That's roughly five billion fish in one year. But more recently, pollock stocks and harvests have plunged as much as 75 percent from their highs, and little is known of this animal's natural history. What is known, says Larry, is that pollock are the mainstay of sea lions and other marine predators.

Antonelis is not so certain about that. And Loughlin says it's speculation to talk of overfishing: "By our assessments, the Bering Sea has 100 million metric tons of fish. The rate of exploitation here is about 20 percent, and many other fisheries have 30 or 40 percent. Biologically, there could be many more fish removed from this system. There's a *lot* of fish out there."

Larry says warning signs began nearly 20 years ago, when islanders first observed that "murre and kittiwake chicks were too weak to hold on to cliff ledges; they fell and died. Then we noticed that sea lions were going after seal pups in greater frequency than ever in living memory. We also noted that when a fur seal pelt was fleshed, the fat taken off, it was so thin that you could practically see light through it. All these things indicated to us that a possible food-stress problem was occurring. We collected the research available and found that seals, sea lions, murres, and kittiwakes *all* were in the pollock food web."

This fact was well known to biologists. "But they didn't look at the connections," Larry insists (though many of them reject the charge). "Each discipline—fish, seals, birds—had its own field data-gathering methodology. They weren't compatible. Computer modeling systems were all different, all highly specialized, seeing a species-by-species orientation." Larry hired an independent biologist who, he says, determined "that pollock stocks were in serious trouble." His report was not acted upon by the North Pacific Fishery Management Council, which determines annual fishing quotas.

A few years later, in 1988, fur seals were declared a depleted species under the Endangered Species Act. NMFS acknowledged that the world population had fallen to 35 or 40 percent of historic highs, but insisted it was stable. It did not recommend any fishing restrictions.

Again Larry appealed to government agencies; again, he says, "nothing happened. No one paid any attention till 1990, when aerial surveys of sea lions from Kenai to Kiska [in the western Aleutians] showed that the population had declined 75 percent from its peaks in the late 1960s. Finally, the University of Alaska held a conference. Attending biologists concluded that more research was needed."

Larry then went international, inviting foreign experts to the Pribilofs. Seabird specialist Alexander Golovkin, head of the Endangered Species Program for the former USSR, surveyed local murres and kittiwakes and found they had declined 80 percent from their 1977 numbers. "He also determined," says Larry, "that all major bird colonies on the Pribilofs—horned puffins, crested auklets, parakeet auklets, tufted puffins, least auklets—*all* of them were in decline! And he concluded that it *definitely* was a food problem. We used to be one of North America's largest bird colonies; we're not any more."

Golovkin also noted that each bird species on the island had its own foraging behavior: Murres are deep divers; kittiwakes are surface feeders. Since both—as well as other species—were declining, he felt that the problem might not be local but Bering Sea-wide. Earlier, he had studied the Barents Sea off Scandinavia and western Russia, where once booming herring and capelin fisheries suddenly went bust. He concluded that overfishing there had sparked a domino-effect collapse of species, fundamentally changing the entire ecosystem.

"The same thing is now happening in the Bering Sea," asserts Larry. "We've documented 15 species now in a state of severe and sustained decline. We started off with six, in 1976. How far do we have to go before everyone recognizes that we've got to look at what the heck is happening?"

Loughlin stresses that he and other scientists simply haven't had enough time or money. The sea lion decline, he says, "wasn't an issue until they dropped to a certain level. When something is about to be listed as threatened, then money falls out of the sky. At what point should we have started turning the spigot and putting money into it? Animals normally vary in numbers; just because an area goes down a little doesn't mean you have to charge ahead and take money away from other areas. It wasn't down across that whole 30 years. It was different parts declining at different rates."

Currently, NMFS classifies the Steller sea lion as "threatened," meaning that its numbers are well below the carrying capacity of the ecosystem. Theoretically, the area has enough habitat and prey to support more sea lions than currently live there. I asked Loughlin about that.

"How do we measure carrying capacity? Nobody has a clue. It's fairly easy when you're on land. You get a measure, by trial and error, that so much foliage means so many deer. But it's very difficult to assess the ocean, this three-dimensional sphere where all the prey move around. The marine sciences aren't sophisticated enough. If the carrying capacity has been lowered—I'm not saying it has, but *if*—you can argue that seabirds and fur seals and everything else out there are stable at the *new* carrying capacity. Can you just keep ratcheting it down and take out what you want? When is all the buffalo grass out of the prairies? The big fear for most people who work in the Bering Sea is, are the Stellers' decline and some seabirds' declines indicative of an ecosystem in peril? We really don't know how to gauge that."

All parties to this running debate—Tom Loughlin and fellow scientists, Larry Merculieff and fellow islanders—are clearly concerned about their region; but they take different approaches, concentrate on different factors, answer to different groups of peers.

Larry comments, "Right now, the Russians are going gangbusters in joint-venture agreements to take out every fish they can, as fast as they can, because they're so desperate for currency. But they did shut down one of their 'nursery zones' in 1992 because they documented a 75 percent decline in pollock." He points out that Presidents George Bush and Boris Yeltsin jointly called for a two-year moratorium on fishing in one key area.

Though such closures aim to protect fish stocks, adds Larry, they actually increase pressure on other areas. At one point, he says, 65 factory trawlers that used to be spread throughout the range were fishing "in *one* zone on the

U. S. side—northwest of this island, 50 miles. *All* of them. We expect that they are going to deplete whatever is left of those stocks, in short order."

Exactly the same plight—too many fishermen and too few fish—currently afflicts the Grand Banks, and other once major fisheries.

In 1991 a task force recommended that 25-mile buffer zones be placed around sea lion rookeries. "That is *not* going to save sea lions," says Larry. "It's a food problem, not a harassment problem. Sea lions should be declared endangered. It's only a matter of time, probably a year or two, before that happens. It hasn't been done yet for *economic* reasons, because once you declare them endangered, the Endangered Species Act comes into play, and you have the whole spotted-owl syndrome—human contact has to be minimized throughout the species' entire migratory range. Since sea lions migrate from Kenai to the Komandorskies [Russia's Commander Islands, near Kamchatka], there'd be tremendous implications for all fishing activities in the Gulf of Alaska, the North Pacific, and the Bering Sea. The economic impact would be *huge.*"

Even Larry, however, faults an "endangered" listing because it views nature species by species, when he thinks the whole ecosystem needs help. And while he ardently believes that pollock overfishing is behind the Bering Sea's numerous wildlife declines, he stresses other factors as well, such as high-seas drift nets. These took a heavy toll—by one official count, 416, 464 seabirds in the North Pacific in 1990—before a United Nations resolution against them took effect in 1992. What was lost besides birds? "One of those things," says Larry, "is bird guano. What's the value of bird poop? It provides phosphates and nitrates that feed into the primary food chain." Losing seabirds by the hundred thousand meant a loss in the productivity of the Bering Sea, and greater stress on the food system.

Larry adds that the Bering Sea problem points up basic flaws in the existing management system. One, he feels, is that it routinely ignores Aleuts and other Native groups.

"Aleuts have lived some 8,700 years in the Bering Sea. We're one of the longest surviving groups of people in a single location in the entire continent. We've lived with and hunted animals and fish and birds. Our people watch the dynamics out here, and have been all these years. But when we try to share our experiences, our knowledge, scientists say it's 'just anecdotal,' therefore of limited use. No one denied we found fur seal pelts all so thin that you could see light through them. No one denies now that seabird chicks were too weak to maintain their holds on cliff ledges. But unfortunately the lay public is disenfranchised from science, because scientists talk in a language that no one can understand. They need interpreters. This disenfranchisement, we think, is ridiculous.

"The test science is put to is unrealistic. It's a legal test: Can you prove beyond a reasonable doubt that this is occurring? No scientist will ever step forward and say, 'Yes, this is so.' They will always equivocate and say, 'Well, we haven't studied this or that. We *think* it might be this.' And that is why you see gigantic failures in management of marine systems around the world—particularly those related to fisheries. You see the collapse in the Barents Sea, the North Sea. Now, we're seeing the Bering Sea in the process of collapse. For the same reason: putting science to an unreasonable test."

Finally, Larry considers the placement of NMFS in Commerce "a clear conflict of interest. Look how much the U.S. Department of Commerce has either loaned to—or underwritten loan guarantees for—the bottom-fishing industry of the Bering Sea. It's in the billions of dollars. If the threat to seals and sea lions is fishing, as it looks like it is, then it's definitely a conflict when the top agency has so much vested interest in that fishery."

Bud Antonelis of NMFS counters: "The department has a lot of goals, and one of them is providing an ecosystem approach to management. You've got to include everything from plankton to marine mammals. Having one agency is much more efficient than having a variety of different agencies."

But, claims Larry, the ecosystem approach has never been instituted; most government scientists continue to study the Bering Sea species by species. Challenged on this point, scientists flatly deny it. Everyone agrees, however, that commercial interests have a history of operating this way.

In the mid-18th century, for example, Russian entrepreneurs took one look at the 1,100-mile-long Aleutian chain and decided that—although nature had left most of it devoid of land mammals—it would make one wonderful fox farm. Its islands were ready-made feedlots, endowed with what seemed an inexhaustible supply of high-protein fox food: millions of nesting seabirds.

Transforming "useless" seabirds into lush, eminently usable fox pelts made perfect business sense, both to Russians and to their American successors. Islands were leased to fox farmers, who sought those with the biggest bird colonies. Before 1941, even the U.S. Fish and Wildlife Service was introducing red and arctic foxes to nearly every rock in the archipelago.

The introductions succeeded only too well. Foxes and rats—the latter brought in accidentally—quickly proliferated at the expense of local seabirds, whose vast colonies nested on unprotected ground. Their huge concentrations encouraged overkill; foxes and rats commonly take more prey than they can eat, caching it for future use. Island after island, colony after colony, species after species, suffered. Populations of Aleutian Canada geese—a diminutive subspecies that breeds only on these islands—were considered close to extinction by the mid-1930s. Little wonder that amateur historian Edgar P. Bailey compares fox farming to the *Exxon Valdez* oil spill as an ecological catastrophe.

The geese were declared endangered in 1973; hunting ceased both in Alaska and in their California winter range. By then Fish and Wildlife had begun the slow, expensive process of removing foxes from some islands. That alone probably wouldn't have saved the Aleutian Canada goose from extinction. What did was human oversight: Three of the smallest and most remote links in the Aleutian chain had been left fox-free. Kiliktagik (near Kodiak), tiny Chagulak (halfway down the archipelago), and Buldir (near the western end) remained small but viable Edens. Chagulak had greater numbers of some seabirds; Buldir boasted more species, and the most geese.

Seabird biologist Ian Jones calls Buldir "the most diverse seabird colony in the Aleutians, and probably in the Northern Hemisphere. What's really unique is its assemblage of small alcids—auklets and murrelets. There're five species of auklets here: least, crested, whiskered, parakeet, and Cassin's. All nest here in the thousands, some in the hundreds of thousands."

Buldir lies so far west that it's actually *east:* longitude 176 east of Greenwich, not far from Attu, Agattu, and the other Near Islands—so named because they are nearest Mother Russia. I went there with Ian and other biologists, including Dan Boone, manager of the Aleutian Islands Unit of the Alaska Maritime National Wildlife Refuge.

Treeless but green, Buldir's rounded hills flowed with wildflowers and thigh-high grass, *Leymus mollis,* also called beach wild rye. Slide-prone cliffs ended in scree slopes and bouldered beaches. Steller sea lions lounged on rocky islets just offshore, while gulls and northern fulmars mewed and wheeled, and eiders quietly negotiated the surf. Puffins milled about on open ground—a sight that just doesn't occur anywhere that foxes do. Bright sun and balmy temperatures belied the Aleutians' usually harsh weather.

Dan's main reason in coming to Buldir was its bonanza of Aleutian Canada geese. Already, Fish and Wildlife had reestablished vanished populations on Nizki and Alaid in the Near Islands group, translocating young geese from Buldir. Now the service hoped to do the same for Kiska and Little Kiska, among the Rat Islands to the east. This approach, Dan explained, should help the species survive any local catastrophe. "Chagulak's population, about 150," he pointed out, "is so small that if birds migrating together get caught in a big bad storm and a bunch go down at sea—say they lose 15 or 20 nesting pairs—that population could nearly be wiped out. That's what we're trying to avoid, why we've established other populations."

Today's goose population hovers around 8,000, enough to improve the bird's status from endangered to threatened. "Now," said Dan, "if Buldir birds were to take a big hit, it wouldn't be good, but it certainly wouldn't be the end of the Aleutian Canada goose." That very day he planned to take some Buldir birds to Little Kiska.

Capturing them sounded relatively easy. Buldir is small, open, and not especially rugged; since geese molt synchronously, whole colonies become flightless at once. I envisioned us scooping up birds in dip nets, at will. But the grass that so thickly blankets much of the island also affords geese infinite cover, and its wave-like texture obscures the lay of the land. Run here and you run blind, as likely to turn an ankle in a hidden stream as you are to bump up against an unseen boulder. In addition, *Leymus mollis* possesses a definite "grain": Go one way and it ripples permissively, go the other and it snarls your legs as kelp ropes an intruding outboard.

Buldir's unpredictable weather dictates that we wear waders and full rain gear, despite the sun. We also carry ten-foot dip nets, with oversize backpacks to carry captured birds, food, and emergency gear. Not exactly a sprinter's outfit, though we will have to run to bag the fleet-of-foot geese. The birds possess another advantage—many have experienced flightnessness and capture attempts before, and they know what to expect.

Dan, however, brings advantages of his own, namely Kyle, Peat, Cap, and Rob. The first three are Scottish border collies, bred to herd sheep and cattle, but trained on domestic ducks. The fourth, Rob Lewis, an animal science professor from Oregon, is the dogs' owner and trainer. I ask why he prefers collies to bird dogs when the quarry, after all, is geese.

"A hunting dog," Rob explains, "puts its nose to the ground and follows. But sheepdogs don't work just by scent. They also have strong visual abilities. We need a dog that can look up, look around, and—even if it doesn't see the bird at first—take a command to swing out wide and eventually come into visual contact with the bird and corral it. That's the herding instinct."

Attend a sheepdog trial, and the border collie's visual orientation is obvious. But on Buldir neither herder nor herdee can see the other because of the grass cover, so the dogs lead with their noses. Rob sends them into the *Leymus*, barking one-word commands. Their response is scattershot, alternately racing in endless circles or porpoising like wolves in deep snow. Not a single goose flushes. Cap, the dominant and oldest member of the team, seems especially frenetic, galloping straight on, then—without command—suddenly dashing off in a different direction.

"He is crazy!" Rob admits with a grin. "And yet, he'll get around fast and won't argue with you, just puts all his energy into it. He's also the hardest dog to read. Because if there are two or three birds, he always focuses on the group. So he's running back and forth, and you think he doesn't have a bird because you don't see any being flushed up.

"See, with people, geese tend to keep moving. They can stay ahead of us all day long. But with dogs, they stay quiet. Even when Cap doesn't find them, his going by causes them to stay put. Kyle and Peat, now, go more into that pointer-type thing, and focus on one bird. Cap really covers an area."

As I watch, Rob's trio gradually settles down and works the patch thoroughly, in tighter and tighter circles. Suddenly, one section of grass riffles oddly, against the wind—or a wing tip breaks the surface—and the dogs home in visually. They do not grab the geese, not usually, but stare them down in their tracks. If a bird chooses to run, the chase is on. But eventually the dogs corner them, one on one. That's when we humans, bent under weighty packs and flailing blindly with dip nets, trot up and bag the birds.

As we head higher, fog and clouds replace the sun. Winds gust to 25 or 30 knots, and for the first time today I'm no longer swearing at my hot, clumsy rain gear. Visibility drops; seagulls resemble geese. Yet we manage to fill all backpacks in a few hours. Forty-eight birds, two to a compartment, six to a pack, head downhill with us. At a workstation near shore each is weighed and measured, then packed off to the FWS research vessel *Tiglax*—its name means "eagle" in Aleut—for the overnight cruise to Kiska.

It has been an incredibly successful day, in which nearly everything worked as planned. And that is the field biologist's ultimate test: What works? Success determines method.

Solid as the rock upon which he stands, a beefy "beachmaster"—a dominant, breeding male fur seal—lords it over his portion of a Pribilof Islands rookery.

FOLLOWING PAGES: Steller sea lions—a half-ton male, with his much smaller females—bask at their rookery on Kagalaska Island.

TOM MELHAM, N.G.S. STAFF; FOLLOWING PAGES: LON E. LAUBER

Seafarers turn cliff-dwellers to reproduce their kind. Horned puffins, or "sea parrots," claw long nest burrows; the beak wanes with summer to winter drab. Crested auklets, dubbed "sea quail" and "plumed knights of the Pribilofs," hide their eggs in rock crevices. The black-legged kittiwake nests on a belly's width of rock shelf. Unlike other gulls—beachcombers and landlubbers—the kittiwake earns the name "seagull." Nesting chores over, it wanders far out to sea.

JEFF FOOTT (BOTH); JOHN & KAREN HOLLINGSWORTH (OPPOSITE)

*C*asting nets upon seas of grass, wildlife biologists Daniel Niven and David Nysewander bag an Aleutian Canada goose on Buldir, in the western Aleutians. They translocate captured birds to other islands, where decades of fox farming killed off natural populations.

*F*rom Mexico to Alaska the song sparrow sweetens the air with its familiar, oft-repeated melody: an overture of single notes, followed by a rush of buzzy notes and trills. The widespread species comes in some 31 varieties, from pale desert races to the big, dark form (opposite) that combs Aleutian beaches for berries, insects, and tiny mollusks and crustaceans. The chocolate lily (left, upper) looks, but does not smell, sweet; it's also known as skunk lily and outhouse lily. Where much else grows low and matty, sea beach senecio, framed by a bridal veil of protective hair, makes a golden splash (lower). On Adak, as on other Aleutian islands, the dark days of rain and fog bring forth a summertime splurge of Nootka lupine and tall buttercup (below).

LON E. LAUBER (BOTH)

*B*ursting surf, snow-seamed rock, and the hovering scud at Adak typify nature's favorite Aleutian pastime: island-bashing. Deep in the earth, the Pacific tectonic plate, sinking below the North American plate, spawned the 1,100-mile-long volcanic chain, still wracked by violent tremors and eruptions. Along this boundary warm and icy sea currents collide, brewing some of the world's foulest weather. It does not deter the handsome emperor goose (opposite). Nearly the entire species—some 80,000 birds—winters in the Aleutians; it breeds along Alaskan and Siberian coasts.

WAYNE LYNCH / DRK PHOTO

*W*alrus pack the beaches of
Round Island, part
of a state game sanctuary
restricted to human visitors,
off limits to hunters and—by
their own choice—to female
walrus. Here, taking on a
pinkish hue as they bask in
sunshine, the bulls rest,
squabble, noise off, and fast
for several days. Then they
slip back into Bristol Bay,
where, like the tufted puffins
(above) and other seabirds
that share the island, they
find sustenance in a rich
foraging ground.

FOLLOWING PAGES: Free,
for the time being, from the
tensions of harem-gathering
and harem-keeping, from
the lethal attentions of ivory
hunters and meat hunters,
the bulls of Round Island
may take their rest in peace.

R. BRANDON / ALASKA STOCK IMAGES (LEFT);
FOLLOWING PAGES: CHARLES KREBS / ALLSTOCK

On Alaska's west coast, where loons splash and cry, the Yukon and Kuskokwim Rivers merge their deltas to form one of the world's richest bird habitats.

FOLLOWING PAGES: Sloughs and ponds cover many of the 26 million acres—22 million federally owned—in the Yukon Delta National Wildlife Refuge.

YUKON DELTA:
Loons and Waterfowl

It is miles wide and inches high, about as flat as land ever gets. It has no trees or roads, just a thin vegetative skin of grass, sedge, and such. Millions of brown, curving sloughs maze it, so dissecting and waterlogging the land that it can be traversed only by floatplane or boat. It is the expansive coastal fringe of the Yukon-Kuskokwim Delta, and it's a world that only a biologist—or a four-year-old—could love.

That's what I decided, anyway, after I stepped off the grounded skiff and instantly plunged knee-deep in mud the color and consistency of chocolate pudding. Great gobbets of the stuff splashed up, covering camera lenses and myself. As I slogged toward the grass-topped bank, the glop grew no shallower, only denser and stickier, like half-set epoxy. My own weight mired me.

Just the effort of raising one foot to take a step drove the other deeper in, making the next step even more challenging. I put everything I had into one huge, convulsive thrust—and my stockinged foot suddenly shot free, leaving its hip boot firmly planted in the muck. There I was, storklike, one foot deeply mired while the other jerked madly about as I struggled both to keep my balance and to get the wayward foot back inside its now-collapsed boot top without first stepping in the goo. Somehow, I succeeded. But yards more remained to be crossed, and I was sinking deeper.

What would Indiana Jones do in such a morass? I asked myself. Of course: stand still, stay calm, and don't struggle. I did all those things—and kept sinking. When it comes to mud, *real* mud, serious mud, staying put simply has no future. I shifted from walking to wading, laboriously pushing through this mud beach rather than attempting to walk *up* it.

Slowly, slowly I neared the grassy shore. Finally I stepped upon it—and my mud-slick boots skidded off in opposite directions, sending me sprawling. I did the only thing a sane, responsible adult could do in that situation: I lay there and laughed, out loud.

One of the world's major deltas, the Yukon-Kuskokwim comprises the bulk of Alaska's southwestern bulge. It is about the size of Missouri, but flat: 70 percent of it lies less than 100 feet above sea level. It is the joint creation of Alaska's two largest rivers, the Yukon and the Kuskokwim, which together drain about two-thirds of the state's 586,412 square miles. It encompasses some two-fifths of the state's coastal wetlands and contains, in fact, the largest single expanse of intertidal habitat in the Western Hemisphere.

Administratively, most of it lies within the bounds of Yukon Delta National Wildlife Refuge, the nation's largest, established in 1980 by the Alaska Lands Act. Water covers nearly a third of its 26 million acres. Its enormously rich wildlife includes various furbearers, shorebirds, seabirds, and marine mammals. But it is best known for its migratory waterfowl.

John Morgart, chief biologist at the refuge, considers the Delta "the single most important waterfowl breeding area in North America. It's one of the greatest producers of ducks in Alaska. We have four goose species, two of which breed virtually only here: the emperor goose and the cackling Canada goose. Also something like 80 percent of the western population of tundra swans. And there are incredible amounts of shorebirds. No one knows how many—thousands, tens of thousands, hundreds of thousands, gosh, maybe millions are produced on the refuge every year."

So it was birds, not mud, that brought me to the outer Delta in spring, specifically to a pintail study area known as Hock Slough. Here I would sample the realities of Delta life and Delta mud, traveling by outboard and on foot with research biologist Paul Flint.

Gaunt as a rail spike and equally tough, Paul steered his skiff through nightmarish scrawls of sloughs that cut the land into innumerable islets, many accessible only at high tide. He got out at one and strode purposefully across the meadowlike surface, eyes constantly scanning. I followed, seeing only grass. Suddenly a thrum and blur of wings burst from what had seemed an ordinary tussock and flew off; Paul dashed to the spot and knelt, then picked up a pale olive egg. He'd found the day's first pintail nest.

Like most female ducks, northern pintail hens are as brown and mottled as dead grass. But shape sets them apart: a long neck and slender body. Pintails nest right on the ground, often on slough edges where currents tend to build up low ridges. They camouflage their nests with grass and are fairly tenacious, flattening into near-invisibility when intruders appear. You almost have to step on them to make them flush.

Quickly Paul examined this nest, candling each egg to check its stage of development by holding it up to the sun and viewing it through a short length of automobile radiator hose that cut out extraneous light. I commented on his rather primitive equipment.

"Hey, this is high-tech," he said with a grin. "Last year we used toilet paper tubes." He passed hose and egg to me; I held them up and saw the dark line of the shell's inner membrane. The shadowy silhouette of a tiny head was pushing against it rhythmically, as regular as a pulsing heart. Of seven eggs, five were viable. Paul noted the ages of each and moved on.

The next nest harbored only scattered shell fragments. "Probably a gull kill," Paul mused. The third also was empty, but papery bits of shell membrane indicated a successful hatch. The fourth nest yielded only two eggs, one of them "star-pipped": Tiny cracks indicated the duckling had begun to break out of its shell.

"Should hatch in about 36 hours," Paul said, pulling a trap from his backpack. It was a clamshell type, consisting of two hinged aluminum rings each about as big as a basketball hoop, strung with netting. He tested a remote-control trigger several times, then placed one ring over the nest and the other flat on the ground, covering both with grass. He wanted to fit successful hens with radios, so now was the time to trap this particular bird.

We nosed up other sloughs, Paul recording the progress of known nests and looking for new ones, at times flushing more nesting hens. I wondered aloud if such disturbances mightn't adversely affect broods.

"Naw," Paul assured me, pointing out that hens regularly leave nests to feed. "Their eggs are virtually bomb-proof. They can really take cooling, even when high storm tides cover them for an hour or so."

Soon it was time to return to our first trap site. A falling tide had grounded the skiff before we could get within range of the remote-control mechanism. We struck out on foot, racing along at a half-crouch like a pair of Groucho Marxes, in hopes the hen wouldn't see us. It was the sloppiest place to be, of course, a child's paradise of black goo.

Suddenly a black turnstone—a shorebird that often plays sentry—cried out its warning whistle; Paul pushed the remote button. A clump of grass ahead fluttered, briefly.

"Got it!" he called, dashing to the nest. Quickly he disentangled a pintail hen from the trap, weighed and measured her, checked her physical condition and probable age, and attached a tiny radio transmitter to her back. Then he gave her a light dose of anesthetic before laying her—rather tenderly, I thought—beside her nest. Those few moments of oblivion, he said, reduce the chance that a hen will abandon her nest after being handled.

Back in camp later in the day, I talked with Barry Grand—a former Louisianan who heads up the pintail project at the refuge—about the Delta's importance as a nesting area.

"Pintails are considered a bird of the prairies," Barry said, "but they're really widespread up here, too. They're the most abundant dabbling duck in Alaska. Their numbers here have been relatively constant—about a million or a million and a half—ever since Alaska started counting ducks, in the '50s."

During that same period, other pintail populations in North America have plunged 66 percent, largely because of drought and agriculture. Even pintails that nest in Alaska are at some risk, as they traditionally winter in California's Central Valley, which has lost 95 percent of its wetlands in the past century. By monitoring population size and nesting success of Alaskan birds, Barry and his co-workers hope to establish information that could be important for wildlife managers. "With the decline of the prairies," he added, "Alaska's become much more important. It's now home to half the breeding pintails of the whole continent." By recent estimates, the Y-K Delta has 300,000 to 800,000 breeding pintails.

"The highest concentrations," said Barry, "are in this coastal fringe where we're working. That's also where the most geese are."

So far, the 12.5-square-mile study area of Hock Slough has yielded more than 550 pintail nests—an unheard-of density for the species. In addition, the average nest has proven to be unusually productive.

"In prairie regions," Barry explained, "about 12 percent of duck nests are successful"—that is, contain at least one egg that hatches. One side of Hock Slough's main channel, he found, had a similar success rate. But the opposite side yielded an astonishing 45 percent, nearly four times as great. That side, Barry noted, was topographically lower than the other, more laced with side sloughs, more susceptible to flooding, more brackish.

At first this puzzled him, because such conditions are hard on newly hatched pintails. For them, highly saline water can be lethal. Why were "low side" nesters so successful? Tagging, radio packs, and careful observations gradually established that pintails quickly leave high-salt areas, once their eggs hatch. Here, at least, they don't have to go far.

"Typically," said Barry, "a brood stays near the nest only a couple of days after hatch. Then they cross the channel and end up in these less saline ponds." Why doesn't a hen nest on the freshwater side to begin with?

The answer, he thinks, involves arctic foxes—bane of ground-nesting coastal birds. Foxes abound on the Delta, especially in drier areas where they can den. Low areas, like one side of Hock Slough, are too wet. "On the highest tides, it's all under two, three inches of water. A fox wouldn't do very well, putting a den on that side. They don't like to get their feet wet. With the network of sloughs here, it's pretty hard to stay dry going from point A to point B—without walking 10 or 12 miles in the process."

Even so, a few foxes have been sighted on Hock Slough's lower side. Their predation at pintail nests is fairly low. When broods leave high-salt areas for fresher ones, they face much higher numbers of foxes. But by then they are no longer stationary and highly vulnerable eggs. So it is that Paul Flint calls Hock Slough "a highway for birds," where species readily shift between the low-predation and high-nutrition sides, as needs change within the nesting season.

Weeks later I visited another Delta research camp, again chartering in by small plane from the regional hub of Bethel. The spongy Y-K was even greener now, textured with freeform patterns of vegetation that seemed swirled on with a brush. Snarly rivers branched into ever stubbier tributaries. Innumerable ponds and oxbows sported floating reefs of algae and pondweeds. Pilot Bruce Larsen asked what line of work I was in, and when I told him, he reacted with enormous enthusiasm: "NATIONAL GEOGRAPHIC? Just about everybody I know who has a subscription to NATIONAL GEOGRAPHIC keeps it in their bathroom. I do. It's the best bathroom reading there is."

Bruce set his plane down on the sluggish, slough-like Tutakoke River and taxied toward a cluster of tents and portable shelters. A regional topographic map, drawn with 50-foot contours, showed almost no contour lines; this place was basically as flat as the sea, and nearly as low.

Here, our quarry would be brant, a sea goose similar in coloration to Canada geese but smaller, its neck patterned with a thin white marking rather than the Canada's white chinstrap. Abundant in the Delta, brant congregate in colonies that are models of togetherness: Whatever they do, from nesting to hatching to molting, they do within a few days of one another. For example, the adults lose their long, flight-essential primary feathers all at once and all at the same time, about a month before their goslings start to fledge. Thus the entire group becomes flightless, for several weeks.

Why would birds evolve such a trait, known as synchronous molting, when it places an entire population at risk? I asked Tutakoke's project leader, research biologist Jim Sedinger. "Because waterfowl can rely on water as an escape, being flightless isn't as big a disadvantage for them as it is for lots of other birds," he answered. "The way most birds molt—dropping one feather at a time on each side—makes flight less efficient. It also takes a couple of months. The consensus is, if you have a way to escape predators anyway— in this case, by swimming—it may be more advantageous to just molt all at once and get it over with." That way, he added, the feathers are in tip-top condition just when the birds need to begin the long fall migration.

To Jim, synchronous molting and colony formation offer yet another advantage. He can easily capture large numbers of birds needed for population and brood studies.

Later I joined him and eight co-workers in a brant search. We rode two skiffs through various sloughs, spotting small congregations here and there, but not enough to make a capture attempt worthwhile. Jim decided to try an area nearer the sea, punctuated by a large, nameless pond.

His strategy was a pincer operation: Surround the area with people, then tighten the human noose and see what you find. The skiffs raced off in opposite directions, dropping people at key locations. The boat I was in headed up a slough that abruptly dead-ended, forcing a detour; another grew so shallow we had to get out and walk the skiff through.

At last we reached our goal, a stretch of shin-high grass near the pond. We spaced ourselves along one side and waited. And waited some more. It seemed an act of faith, for I hadn't seen a single brant yet.

Ahead, the grass billowed slightly in the breeze. A distant section seemed to blur and waver, like asphalt on a hot day. Then it grew darker. I looked through my telephoto. Hundreds of brant were bursting through the grass and running our way! But soon they veered off, aiming for a major gap in our human net: the pond. A few of us ran into the water, and the birds slowed to a standstill. Why didn't they go back to wherever they'd come from?

Now I saw why: About half a mile beyond the brant, a human form suddenly arose from the grass sea. Then a second, even more distant, popped up, followed by still more in between. The other skiff-load of biologists had arrived. They'd stayed low till now, closing the circle at a crouch before standing up and becoming instantly visible, for miles. Had I been a brant, I'd have run, too. But they were surrounded; all that remained was for us to slowly tighten the noose, deterring breakout attempts with an arm wave or flick of a cap, driving the birds before us like sheep. That's how ten people rounded up more than a thousand birds in only twenty minutes.

Strangely, the brant seemed to grow more docile as we contracted around them. Only six people ringed them now; the other four had retrieved stakes and netting from the skiffs, and were rigging a corral nearby. We stood and the brant stayed, murmuring as they watched us calmly

Then the real work began: Jim and three others, seated on folding chairs amid arrays of colorful, inch-wide plastic leg bands and other paraphernalia of the field biologist, formed a receiving line. Several "runners" grabbed two or three birds at a time from the corral and ferried them first to the seated foursome, then to a holding pen. Two recorders scribbled in notebooks as the four processors hectically measured, weighed, banded, sexed, and tagged each bird, shouting out findings in rapid-fire. It was bedlam: birds everywhere, coming and going for hours, amid a nonstop babel of voices.

How the two note-takers kept the different voices and data straight, I couldn't fathom. But they did. The frenzied production line banded and measured nearly 800 adult birds in about five hours—and tagged a sampling of goslings as well. Processed birds went to a holding pen, then were released all at once. They headed straight for the water.

A few goslings strayed—and glaucous gulls swiftly moved in, picking them up, then dropping and savagely pecking them. Far more would have succumbed if the local population of black turnstones had not attacked the much larger gulls and driven them off. Tiny but agile and totally unafraid, the highly territorial turnstones were defending their own nests; the goslings were lucky beneficiaries.

One evening back in camp, three Yupik Eskimo youths in an open boat stopped by to chat. Within minutes, a rabbit emerged on a nearby mudflat, as it had every night about this time. The trio of visitors immediately dashed to their boat for rifles. Boom! Boom! Boom! They fired at least a dozen rounds—far more than the meat of any rabbit was worth—finally shattering two of its legs. They ran to it and clubbed it, coming back full of grins and pride. "I *told* you I hit it," one said, beaming. He offered it to us. We declined. Eventually he tossed it in the boat, without gutting it. A few minutes later they were blasting away again, at sandpipers on the far shore.

Set against Alaska's vast size, of course, what is a single rabbit or sandpiper? The three kids were just on a lark, being kids, having fun.

Wasteful hunting, however, isn't unusual in this state; examples occur everywhere. A North Slope camp cook tells of a neighbor who shot enough ducks to fill eight garbage cans—in springtime, during nesting season—and he was not the only villager to do so. Many birds were never eaten. Elsewhere, a pilot confides that he's seen ptarmigan "stacked five feet deep in a corner of a house—rotting. All this stuff about 'we only shoot to eat' is bull."

For people who live off this land, Alaska's brutal climate and the migratory nature of its wildlife can mean prolonged lean times. Native Alaskans survived and even prospered over countless generations by taking maximum advantage of game opportunities whenever they occurred. Each fall, huge and well-organized harvests of salmon, caribou, and seals took place; most meat was put up for the arduous winter. Spring's arrival of waterfowl often represented the first chance for fresh meat in months, and people responded eagerly, taking both nesting birds and eggs. Federal law forbade this in 1919, but in fact remote villages were beyond its reach. The wildlife endured, for the take was small compared to the whole.

But today the amounts in these equations have shifted. Alaska's human population has swelled ninefold in this century: to almost 600,000. More hunters exist today—and they have up-to-date weaponry, outboards, nets, snowmobiles, and more. For Native hunters, says Jim Sedinger, not only the hardware has changed; so too has the hunting ethic.

"I've talked to older guys in the villages; when they went hunting, they took maybe five or six shotgun shells—and they were supposed to come back with five or six birds. If you came out here for a week of hunting, you made damn sure you had a lot of meat when you finished. And that requires more discipline than what's required now."

Today, large-scale Native hunts continue, with modern weapons and conveniences, and in some instances they seem to have strained nature's ability to resupply. All four goose species that nest on the coast suffered dramatic declines in recent decades, evidently because of overhunting, either by Native Alaskans on the spring nesting range or by sport hunters on the birds' winter ranges. The entire world population of cackling Canada geese nests on the Delta; in only 20 years, it plunged 90 percent. Pacific whitefronts fell 80 percent, Delta-wide, while emperors suffered a 70 percent drop. And brant —the Delta once boasted half the world's brant—plummeted to only 10,000 breeding pairs by 1986.

"The only thing they had in common," Jim Sedinger told me, "is that they nested on the Delta. There wasn't any loss or degradation of habitat here. Subsistence harvests *had* to have played a role."

While hunting pressures increased on Delta geese, so did fox predation, largely because of man. Low fur prices and a lull in trapping meant that more foxes survived, while the hunting of marine mammals provided them with a food windfall as carcasses washed ashore. Fox populations boomed.

In 1986 the Fish and Wildlife Service reacted by trapping foxes on the Delta. It had already called for "voluntary cessation" of egging, and had tightened restrictions on sport hunting of cacklers, whitefronts, and brant. Today, all but emperors have bounced back. Brant have rebounded especially well, said Jim. "On the Delta now, we're back close to or maybe in excess of what was here in the early '80s. We've seen a three- or four-fold increase in some colonies."

The lesson, he and other biologists think, is clear: Subsistence hunting must be limited in some ways, if the resource is to continue to flourish. "We don't have good data on the magnitude of the subsistence harvest. Surveys are done, but they're voluntary, in randomly selected villages and randomly selected households. You're asking people to report all their hunting activities, and they're afraid of getting into trouble with the law."

Jim would like to see the law changed so that quotas can be set for the spring hunt and the waterfowl population managed openly.

If you take birds in spring, of course, the effect is multiplied. Shoot one adult female, and you've got a single goose for the pot. But you're actually taking six or eight birds, since you're also depriving the population of all the goslings she might have produced that season.

Because Jim has worked closely with waterfowl since 1977, affiliated with the University of Alaska's Institute of Arctic Biology, you might expect him to be firmly opposed to spring hunting. But like many other wildlife biologists in Alaska, he strongly believes that both sport and subsistence hunting have their place.

"I think subsistence hunting needs to be regulated, but I also think it's important for the maintenance of Native culture. In a lot of Native villages there's been tremendous social deterioration. Subsistence hunting is one of the positive things that villages have. It's an important part of the lifestyle and it needs to be an ongoing activity. Because you don't see too many alternatives out here. There're never going to be auto manufacturing plants or those kinds of jobs. And the loss of a subsistence hunting ethic is detrimental, because all the things that go along with being a successful hunter—discipline and those kinds of things—go with it. There's nothing to replace it."

Tender cargo: Black brant goslings squirm in the arms of volunteer Tim Obritschkewitsch as he carries them to a banding station.

FOLLOWING PAGES: Like cowboys herding cattle, biologists ease black brant—rendered flightless by seasonal molting—into net corrals.

*B*irds, birds, birds. *"The single most important waterfowl breeding area in North America," one refuge biologist calls the Delta. A short-eared owl (opposite) nests in tall marsh grass. Alaska supports half the continent's breeding pintails (right); loss of habitat elsewhere has led to a 66 percent decrease in the species. Red-necked phalaropes (below) sometimes "spin" while feeding, creating a vortex that draws food up from the bottom.*

CHLAUS LÖTSCHER; NATALIE B. FOBES (OPPOSITE); WAYNE LYNCH / DRK PHOTO (UPPER)

*W*ith tags on its neck and legs, an emperor goose takes off from Delta waters. In recent years, populations of all species of geese have fallen here,

partly because of overhunting. Thanks to conservation efforts, all have lately begun to recover except the emperor, still down by 63 percent.

*P*erpetual threat to ground-nesting birds, the red fox—with plentiful food and only man as an enemy—thrives. Yawning, scratching, chasing tails—the life of a red fox kit here seems carefree. Red foxes occur naturally nearly everywhere in Alaska, though on some islands the population results from fox-farming operations early in the century. Arctic foxes fill the predator's niche along the coast. "Vixens" and "dogs" mate late in winter in dens, usually on the side of a knoll. Four kits commonly make a litter. Adults have a large and expressive repertoire of howls, barks, and whines. With their silky pelts, they are important to the fur industry in Alaska, and each year trappers take several thousand. The price of pelts affects the number of foxes on the Delta—and ultimately the number of birds: As the price of fur falls, trappers stay home—and the fox population grows.

GARY SCHULTZ; ANIMALS ANIMALS / JOHNNY JOHNSON

*M*ajestic and graceful, tundra swans take to the air over the Delta. Swans from here migrate in family units or small flocks hundreds or thousands of miles, at altitudes of 5,000 feet and speeds of 50 miles an hour. Until recent years they were called whistling swans, for the sound of their powerful wings beating in flight. These swans' northern home, the Yukon-Kuskokwim Delta, receives water and sediments from nearly two-thirds of Alaska, creating some two-fifths of the state's coastal wetlands.

A careful parent, a red-necked grebe nests on a floating raft it and its mate have built (opposite). White eggs have taken on a brown tint from the decaying vegetation. The birds' impressive courtship rite features synchronous swimming and duets of tuneless rattles; reddish neck spots disappear after mating season. Grebes are among the 50 or so species of shorebirds and waterbirds—numbering in tens of millions—that nest each year in the Delta or use it for resting and foraging during migration. Chicks (below)—like aircraft being refueled in midair—get fed by one parent while riding on the back of the other.

FOLLOWING PAGES: Lesser Canada geese flank a gosling armada 19 strong; four or five eggs per nest are more common. Many of the Delta's Canada geese winter in the disappearing wetlands of California's Central Valley.

The mouths of babes—yearling wolves, actually—gape with playful menace. Their social sparring presages adult dominance rituals and skirmishes with other packs.

FOLLOWING PAGES: Sable Mountain's forbidding face serves as "escape terrain" for Dall sheep: wary, agile climbers—and the only white sheep in the wild.

THE INTERIOR:
Wolves and Sheep

You don't need to be a rocket scientist to catch mountain sheep, but it doesn't hurt. Not that Wayne Heimer puts himself in that category. A sheep biologist with Alaska's Department of Fish and Game, Wayne has been chasing Dall sheep for nearly 20 years. This pure white, slightly smaller cousin of the Rocky Mountain bighorn is so quick and agile, he told me, that it routinely eludes conventional capture devices such as projectile-thrown nets, and even net guns, which use blank rifle cartridges to propel folded, umbrella-like nets.

"We tried them, but they're just too slow; the animals got away. See, a bullet—or a net projectile—starts slowing down as soon as it leaves the gun barrel. But a rocket, where you've got fuel *inside*, keeps going faster and faster." Thus Wayne's solution to his sheep "problem": rocket nets.

All the while he spoke, he was jamming plastic sacks of propellant designed for 105-millimeter military mortars into homemade rockets: foot-long chunks of 2.5-inch steel tubing, sealed at one end. The other end had a screw-on cap. To load, you unscrew the cap, plop in the sack—making sure that the two wires leading from the propellant protrude through an exhaust port—then replace the cap. Then you connect the wires to cables that lead to a dry-cell battery. Simple.

Wayne had attached four rockets at regular intervals to a long edge of a 60-by-40-foot net, mounting them atop metal stakes. These in turn over-looked a low, pawed-over bubble of dirt ten or fifteen yards across, partway up a green mountain ridge. This, he explained, was a mineral lick; it was bare because as many as 1,200 Dall sheep regularly come here from miles around, to feast on the mineral-rich soil.

Our campsite was downhill beside the silvery, rock-filled riffle called Granite Creek.

Granite Creek lies in the Interior—that vast swath of inland Alaska that is bounded north and south by the Brooks and Alaska Ranges. Its eastern border is Canada; west sprawls the Y-K Delta. It is a land of sweeps, often forested, often rolling, laced with rivers and bogs and lakes.

Wayne, two volunteers, and I had taken some 14 hours to cover the 140 miles from Fairbanks to Granite Creek. The first hundred miles had been easy: paved roads to Delta Junction, just north of the Alaska Range. The last 40 were pure adventure, following an insubstantial dirt track. Wayne had equipped us with four-wheelers commonly called all-terrain vehicles, or ATVs: motorcycles with training wheels.

"Plan on mud," Wayne warned us. Thanks to a late and sudden breakup, the nearby Tanana River was in flood. We started off in boreal forest, dodging trunks and branches and broken roots sharp enough to puncture even our balloon tires. Woods soon gave way to a plainlike expanse— the Army had cleared it for parachute training, Wayne said—then to scrub forests of spindly spruces and willows, and to rolling stretches of tundra. The willows were in full bloom, their delicate, fuzzy flowers reminiscent of coral polyps. Other blossoms—tiny but great in number—gave a lavender cast to the tundra. Beyond stood the Alaska Range, each snowclad peak massive and abrupt and separate from its neighbors, unlike the jagged crush of the Brooks Range. Serenity personified—save for the yammering of our ATVs.

Mud-filled wallows, steep hills, and branch-dodging continually challenged us; the ATVs responded. So well, in fact, that even a greenhorn like me soon felt the machine's addictive lure, born of near misses and the sheer exhilaration that comes from barrelling full-bore through what at first seems impassable. I found myself steering dead-on for the most treacherous places.

Then a mudpit swallowed my bike nearly to the handlebars. Luckily, Dave Larson, the volunteer just ahead of me, noticed my absence and returned to help rock the bike free of its sticky grave. A few more miles of muddy ruts followed, then a sustained hill-climb took us to road's end. It had been a seven-hour mudbath; we looked like bikers from hell.

We parked the ATVs and set off along game trails. It felt good to walk—and to hear again. Dave, a birder, waved me off just as I was about to step unknowingly on a white-tailed ptarmigan, its speckled plumage and football shape perfectly mimicking the surrounding rocks. Two and a half hours passed before we reached Wayne's field cabin near the mineral lick.

The next day brought a crash course on Dall sheep behavior. The nearby lick, Wayne explained, provides sheep with their regular fix of calcium and magnesium. Dall sheep lose as much as half their bone thickness each winter, metabolizing calcium from their bodies to make up for seasonal lacks in their diet. And spring's new growth complicates the calcium problem, said Wayne. "As all this stuff greens up, it gets just sky-high in phosphorus. If you're a ruminant and you eat phosphate, you have to balance that ionically. Calcium's a good way to do that. Sheep, I think, come here to get a big mouthful of calcium, so they can dump the phosphate and get their skeletal systems back up."

In addition, the mineral-rich dirt provides magnesium, necessary for proper muscle function. Indeed, the lick is so essential that sheep keep coming, even after repeated nettings. Wayne outlined their normal schedule:

"From four in the afternoon till four in the morning, the dominant activity in the Alaska Range is lying around." Sounded good to me. "By 4:30 a.m. most of the sheep are up, moving about and eating. That's usually when they come here. People call it a 'salt lick,' but it's really a 'dirt eat.' They gobble it by the mouthful, like ice cream. Typically they'll eat for an hour, then go away and lie down a couple of hours, then come back and eat dirt for a half an hour, then lie around for another hour. Then they leave. It's always an early morning activity; they *never* come by late in the day or at night."

Two days in a row dawn solid gray, with drizzlies, and for some reason the sheep keep their distance. Dave and John Abrams—the other volunteer—and I opt for a day hike. Lichens turn granite outcrops slick in the gray rain. We don't see many birds, but we hear them. Dave identifies species after species by its call. A rock ptarmigan flushes. Ground squirrels rise from boulders amid spongy, wet muskeg. The appearance of a pika—more elusive than ground squirrels—elates John, who is an avid sheep hunter and outdoorsman. We spot no sheep, but lots of wolf scat and some bear sign.

Back in camp, I head for my tent. Soon John comes to announce that three ewes are at the lick, and Wayne wants to try for them. I hurry to join the group, glancing at a watch: 6 p.m. Wayne looks at me and grins. "They *never* come in the afternoon," he says.

Before we begin the hundred-yard hike up to the lick, Wayne tells us: "Just act sloppy. Take it easy. Don't look at their eyes, or they'll spook."

We string out and adopt a slow, almost wallowing gait, pausing here and there, looking from side to side or back, anywhere but at the sheep. We must seem a caravan of bums locked in a muscatel haze as we straggle up-slope. This can't possibly work, I tell myself. But every time I sneak a fleeting peek uphill, the sheep remain. At first they go into their "alarm posture"—heads up, rigid and watchful—then go back to idly grazing the dirt. Sooner than I expect we're at Wayne's blind, a small A-frame near the edge of the lick. The three sheep, about to be joined by a yearling, are nervous.

"BRRRRRRP." Wayne lets out what sounds like a very low, loud, long belch. "BRRRRRRRP!" It's the mating call of the ram, he explains later.

In the tiny blind, Wayne goes from slob role model to efficiency expert. "You ready?" he whispers. He holds a bared wire end in each hand, inches from the terminals of the dry cell. "Five. Four. Three. Two..."

"Hold it!" I whisper hoarsely, adjusting camera and light meter.

Seconds later the wires touch—BOOOOM—and the four rockets arch over the sheep, carrying the net in a curve as neat as a waterfall. All three ewes instantly tangle. The yearling, just out of range, flees uphill.

We race to the ewes, restraining them to prevent self-injury as Wayne slips sleeve-like blindfolds through the net and over their muzzles. Hobbles of nylon webbing lash their feet together. The ewes take it well, their breathing growing more regular. As the net is peeled farther back, a mild touch reassures the blinded animals. No cuts, no broken bones, no pain.

There is one loss, however: Their once brilliantly white coats are now gray as those of bighorns, coated with the lick's dark, bentonite-rich soil. All three receive quick injections of a veterinary drug that Wayne calls "sheep Valium." He explains: "It's a mood leveler; they can do all the things they regularly do, they just don't want to as much."

He quickly assesses each animal's reproductive condition and general health. Annular rings on horns tell the age. Wayne feels carefully for lumpy jaw, a bacterial infection that can lead to tuberculosis-like abcesses in the mandible and a shortened life. He also takes blood samples, measures body and leg lengths, girth, and—like a country doctor—checks the tongue. "They're in really poor condition," he notes, "thinner than usual."

Each gets a nylon-and-plastic collar, rivetted around the neck. These stay for life, their numbers and letters enabling Wayne to track them as birders do birds. Then the blindfolds come off, the hobbles fall slack—and soon the sheep are gone, trotting up to high ground. We refold the net and re-arm the rockets, leaving the lick ready for our next assault.

By this time, other sheep have appeared. Despite the rocket firing, despite our capturing their sisters, these late arrivals dare ever nearer, some to within 15 feet. Are they just curious? Stupid? Or so secure in their speed and agility that they simply have no fear?

Dall sheep linger at the heart of a controversy that has enveloped Alaska for decades: wolf control. Historically, pioneers reacted to wolves much as they did in the lower 48—they killed them. Some wanted to encourage the sheep and other game species, others to protect livestock. Bounties and poisoning became commonplace; later, so did aerial shooting. For decades, the U. S. Fish and Wildlife Service sent its own staff on intense wolf hunts, and encouraged independent pilots and hunters to eliminate more wolves by offering them free ammunition. Even the Park Service practiced wolf control during the 1940s and '50s, even in Mount McKinley National Park (enlarged and named Denali in 1980).

During the same period, renowned naturalist Adolph Murie began studying wolves and other animals there. While he admitted that these predators were "the chief check" on Dall sheep, he concluded that they were good for the ecosystem, because they weeded out the unfit. The work of Murie and others fostered a new image of old Lobo: that he was—as Wayne Heimer puts it—"a biological toothbrush that would scrub up the ecosystem."

Alaska's Department of Fish and Game took over and, he adds, "was really in the forefront of civilizing the wolf from predator to game animal, to icon. With the coming of statehood, in 1959, wolves became a big-game animal, as well as a fur animal. Major wolf research programs and protection programs began. We did away with bounty and den hunting and poisoning."

In 1972, the state banned aerial hunting for sport. The wolf population in the Tanana Flats area south of Fairbanks had been especially suppressed, Wayne recalls.

"We had bunches of moose. Human harvest picked up, and wolf abundance increased. Between the wolves and us, we ate almost everything."

State officials reacted with concentrated wolf-kill programs. "Sheep stabilized immediately," recounts Wayne. "Then they grew, re-establishing their numbers. Wolves more than re-established *their* numbers, and now sheep are down to maybe half where they once were."

Again the wolf's image had changed. Says Wayne, "They're opportunistic." But he adds that, usually, sheep are not the wolf's main course. "Typically we associate wolves with more resilient and stable prey: moose, which are big and have multiple births and occur in large herds, or caribou, which are typically very abundant. When wolves get down to eating sheep—and I think that's what it comes to—there's *something* going on."

Indeed, the Brooks Range harbors perhaps half of the state's Dall sheep, and they have thrived in spite of resident wolves and the far north location. Problems begin when populations expand into foothills and other marginal areas where their escape tactics don't work as well, giving wolves a greater advantage. Areas like foothills near the Tanana Flats.

Here, sheep do well only as long as wolf control keeps down predation, or other prey species remain abundant enough to relieve the pressure on sheep. During the particularly hard winter of 1992-93, caribou fled the Flats—and local citizens began to call for more wolf control.

In late 1992, Fish and Game, which oversees all hunting in the state, unveiled its Strategic Wolf Management Plan. This called for selective measures that included aerial hunting in a few areas—shooting from airplanes and helicopters—as well as a "land and shoot" technique after tracking the animal from the air.

Fish and Game managers saw the proposed use of helicopters as a humane and efficient way to control wolves in difficult terrain. But to critics, it suggested Vietnam-like visions of Huey gunships cruising the tundra. Tour and conservation groups threatened boycotts; Governor Walter J. Hickel soon took action. The plan was abandoned for at least 1993, and a "wolf summit" was convened in January to debate the issue.

While wolf-lovers celebrated, however, wolf biologists agreed that the plan would actually have benefited most wolves in the state.

David Mech, well known for more than 35 years of wolf research both in the lower 48 and in Alaska, explains that the plan "would have killed *fewer* wolves each year than have been killed in past years, because although they were going to control wolves in one tiny part of Alaska—3 percent—they were closing the season on wolves in a much larger area than they had before. They were *increasing* total protection for wolves by 50 percent. But you didn't read that. The media created the impression that they were trying to destroy all wolves in Alaska."

The purpose of the program, he says, was "to produce caribou and moose for the hunters. You may not agree with that, and that's fine. But it will work; you can kill off wolves for a few years, increase the moose and caribou, increase the harvest by human hunters—then let the wolves come back. Where you have a higher number of moose and caribou, you'll get a higher number of wolves. That's the intent, and that's what they've shown scientifically they can do. You can disagree with the ethics of it, but that's personal opinion."

Bob Stephenson, a Fish and Game biologist with more than two decades of wolf research to his credit, points out that Alaska removed the wolf from the category of pest. Hunters and trappers take 11 to 14 percent of the state's wolves in a year, with no apparent ill effects.

"This level of harvest," he says, "is well below levels that would be required to reduce the overall wolf population." Over the past 20 years, he adds, wolves actually have increased slightly in numbers and repopulated some areas—such as the Kenai Peninsula—from which they were extirpated earlier in the century, recovering nearly all their historic ranges. Current estimates place the statewide population between 5,900 and 7,200 animals, aggregated in perhaps 600 or 700 packs. How does that compare to earlier eras? Bob Stephenson can't say, because no organized census existed prior to the 1970s. He doubts the widely published figure of 15,000 wolves.

Sheep biologist Wayne Heimer adds, "If you've got a high prey density, wolves or other predators will not have a big impact on it; there will be some sort of equilibrium. But if you displace that equilibrium to a low level—we call it the 'predator pit'—it's like an eddy trapping the prey population. Once in the eddy, or pit, some species take a long time to recover, while others do not seem able to rebound without help from man."

Over time, wolves in such a situation will "overgraze" their territory. Then their population falls to lower levels. That's fine from nature's perspective. But many biologists are employed as wildlife managers, who seek to minimize population booms and busts.

Wolves, Bob comments, are an especially resilient species. "Most females breed pretty much every year, after they're two years old. Pup survivability is high; by far the majority of pups that come out of the den in June are still there in November."

Normally, he says, pack sizes remain fairly stable, with many young wolves and some adults dispersing to other areas. Once Bob plotted the general location of about 150 packs that have been studied, with radio-collars, in Alaska and the Yukon since 1975. Then he plotted the long-range dispersals. It looked as if someone had spilled a box of spaghetti on a map of the state: a maze of lines crisscrossed it, bridging all geographical and political boundaries. "Wolves blast off all over the place. Each year thousands of them disperse in what seem to be random directions, moving 500 miles or more to other regions. In a sense," he concludes, "most wolves in Alaska belong to a single population that is intimately connected with a large population in northwestern Canada." Curtail packs here and there, this suggests, and others always will replace them.

Authorization for wolf control lies in Alaska's constitution, which declares that wildlife "shall be utilized, developed and managed on the sustained yield principle." To many Alaskans, game is a resource to be relied on regularly; they are understandably reluctant to let "natural" systems have long-term and at times dramatic population swings.

Still, even some game managers admit that a few of their schemes turned out to be—as one said candidly— "trophy-size" blunders. Another said of a wolf-control program in Nelchina Basin, south of the Alaska Range: "Money was spent there and wolves were killed, but wolves weren't the problem. It was *bears*."

Fish and Game once encouraged hunters to take less-than-mature Dall rams, and even ewes, in the mistaken belief that these practices would spur sheep productivity. Instead, they left flocks with sexually mature but socially inexperienced "teenagers" in charge. Lambing fell dramatically.

Yet another Fish and Game project, ideal in theory, led to increased hunting of cow moose. But the managers overestimated the ability of moose to respond, and they underestimated the impact of bears and wolves. Admits Wayne Heimer, "It really gets your attention when you see a stack of three or four rams just lying in the snow, wolf tracks all around. But how important is it in the big picture?"

The big picture, of course, is what wildlife managers strive to bring into focus, most effectively through trial and error and research. Alaska's big picture includes more than wildlife, and can be especially frustrating. In 1980, ANILCA complicated things by splitting the bulk of Alaska into a pastiche of private, state, and federal lands and giving preference to subsistence rights. In national forests, wildlife refuges, and newly created parks, it allowed subsistence hunting, fishing, trapping, wood-gathering, and other traditional activities. Of the national parks, only the old portions of Denali, Katmai, and Glacier Bay stand as pure sanctuaries committed to preserving natural systems without interference unless a native species is seriously threatened.

Of this trio, only Denali harbors all "Big Five" major game species: brown bear, wolf, moose, caribou, and sheep. These and other attractions explain why some people call it *the* wildlife park of Alaska.

Since the mid-1980s, park biologists Tom Meier and John Burch have been radio-collaring wolves to study their movements throughout Denali. The number of wolves there has doubled in that time, to a high of perhaps 180 animals, grouped in as many as 16 packs. Against Alaska's 7,000 wolves statewide, that may not sound like many, admits Tom.

"There's lots of wolves everywhere between here and the Atlantic Ocean, all across Canada. But *this* is the only big place I know of in the world where most wolves don't in the end get killed by people. In Denali, wolves mostly are killed by other wolves. So you can make the argument that this is *the* place to study the population, to see what happens in the absence of human interference. The other argument you could make is, hey, if this is the only place they're being left alone, well, let's *leave* them alone."

Among biologists, of course, the former argument won out long ago. Tom and John's collaring operation at Denali is a natural extension of Murie's observational work here, begun 40 years before. At their office in park head-quarters, they pointed to a wall map bristling with map pins. Each color, Tom explained, designated a particular pack; each pin, a different sighting.

"That pack up there with the white pins, they founded the red-pin pack, the black-pin pack to the north, the greens to the southwest, the pinks just east of there—they're all offspring from one pack. That's what impresses me after six years: how much change there is in the whole system."

Over that span of time, he added, six or seven packs died out.

"Not from human cause. They were killed by wolves—not eaten, just killed. We haven't had any evidence of wolves being killed by their own pack; it's always the next-door neighbors, a territorial thing. But the weirdest thing is that we found half a dozen cases of wolves being *accepted* into a strange pack. Here they are, killing each other at a great rate, and then a totally strange wolf comes by and they take it in! It's hard to figure."

Like humans, wolves possess a complex and dynamic social structure, one that remains imperfectly known to us. Bob Stephenson's "spaghetti map" showed that, though wolves are strongly territorial, they often cross enormous distances, at times through challenging and unknown terrain. Tom and John wanted to know why.

They were especially intrigued by the "Little Bear" wolf pack—named for a creek they frequented in Denali Park. The researchers had radio-collared three of the pack's eleven members, but this spring the entire pack abruptly dropped out of sight and sound for nearly a month. Tom and John went airborne to continue their search, and invited me along.

The pilot put his Cessna in a slow circle at 5,000 feet, then again at 6,000 feet, but nothing came over the headsets. Ahead rose the spine of the Alaska Range, totally dominated by slope-shouldered Mount McKinley, at 20,320 feet the continent's high point. We headed west-southwest, toward McKinley and climbing. Below, the main park road traced a tan thread across foothills and through the fanlike braids of the Toklat River's east fork. The broad swath of Muldrow Glacier poked its gritty and fractured tongue from McKinley's base. Gray glacial flour choked streams of icemelt; pothole lakes gaped clear and green, amid forests and meadows alive with spring's blush.

A few bleeps came over the headsets—but from caribou, Tom said, checking the frequency. On we flew, leaving the park for equally rugged state lands. McKinley stands near a major bend in the Alaska Range, which here veers from an east-west axis to a north-south one. We were heading southwest now, along the wall. Below sprawled forests streaked by narrow streams and dotted only occasionally by cabin or airstrip, remnants of homestead grants. On a hunch, Tom directed the pilot toward the south fork of the Kuskokwim River.

Now limpid emerald-green lakes spatter the land. The color is brilliant, electric; it seems more suited to Disney's palette than to nature's. Tom and John say they have spotted lone wolves here before, park wolves that had strayed this far south and west, but never an entire pack. As we cross a side stream, Tom announces quietly: "We got it."

A second beep follows, then silence. We circle for altitude. The country is vast, expansive and convoluted, rugged with ridges and cross-ridges. At 8,400 feet the beeps return, behind us, slightly to the right. The pilot heads for them, dropping fast. Trees loom up from washboard ridges. Suddenly, six loping, yellowish shapes burst from the forest fringes and bound back in again, melting into the shadows. I see them for only part of a second. We circle three, four times more. John spots some motion, then nothing. The radio reassures us the wolves were not a mirage, but we will not see them again today.

A map check shows that we have flown nearly two hundred miles.

"That's no farther than they were the last time we sighted them," Tom says. "They're just on the wrong side of the biggest mountain range on the continent, is all."

Later, he continues to marvel at the pack's mobility.

"They crossed the range in the second of very few, rare passes that they could have got through. I assume they didn't just climb a mountain but found a reasonable path. Why did they do it? It's a new behavior pattern. They're not supposed to move around like this. But there they are.

"They didn't look hungry. I suspect they didn't have pups; that's usually what holds a pack in one place in summertime, the den and the pups. None of those we saw were breeding animals, they were all just yearlings or so. For all we know there could be a female back in a den, somewhere. Last year this group had two litters; eleven pups last fall. Why they would go from having two litters to having none, I don't know.

"They could get into trouble, poking up these valleys and crossing a mountain range. They could run across ten other wolves and be killed. I guess I would be surprised now, if they came back, because they just can't make a beeline for home; they'd have to go right over Mount McKinley."

I closed my eyes, reliving again and again the pulsing, bounding, split-second image of the "lost" pack in the trees, on its way somewhere. It sure didn't seem lost. Would they stake out a new territory and proliferate, or would they perish? Tom and John couldn't say. At least their species, for now, seemed destined to endure.

FOLLOWING PAGES: A Dall sheep nuzzles and nurses her lamb. Ewes give birth alone, in a rugged place, chosen for its safety.

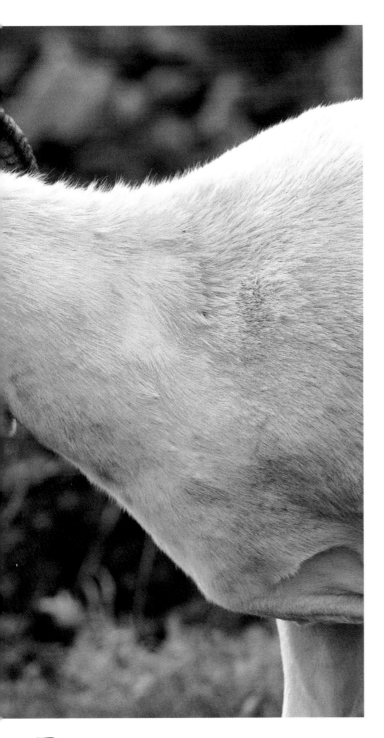

*D*all rams charge and butt each other, horns clashing, in a contest for dominance. Such battles occur year round, most often before mating season. "Full-curl" horns show that a ram has survived seven or eight years—that is, four or five winters away from the usual life span in the wild.

*L*one marmot does sentry duty outside its burrow, hidden beneath a many-tiered warren of talus in the range locally called the Granite Mountains. Related to squirrels, marmots hibernate most of the year, emerging in April or May to find food and mates. Like prairie dogs, they live in colonies and sound alarms to each other when danger threatens. Ground squirrels (far left and left), pikas, voles, lemmings, and other small mammals occur throughout interior Alaska, feeding on various plants and falling prey to red foxes (left), weasels, marten, wolves, and brown bears.

Interior flatlands hold uncounted lazy streams. At right, nameless waters thread Denali State Park, neighbor to the renowned national sanctuary. Below, a mink pauses alertly on a hollow log, probably its den. Mink feed on fish— and anything else they can kill—as avidly as trappers take them. Along the streams, beavers build their dams and lodges—and humans set their traplines in season. All but a few public lands permit trapping and subsistence hunting for rural residents.

*T*rumpeter swans flourish today as living trophies for conservation: In 1932, biologists counted just 69 wild trumpeters in the world. Thanks to vigorous protective measures, these swans now number in the thousands. At right, a vigilant mother watches one of her cygnets nibble on horsetail, a wild grass. World's largest waterfowl, adult trumpeters can consume 20 pounds of aquatic vegetation a day. Ninety percent of them nest each spring in Alaska's marshes.

MICHAEL DEYOUNG / ALASKA STOCK IMAGES (ABOVE); AL GRILLO (BELOW)

*A*utumn glory signals the advent of winter severity. Aspen leaves (left) brighten the ground, while a rock ptarmigan (below) boasts the first hints of its snowy winter plumage. Come snowfall, the lynx (right), Alaska's only native cat, will rely on its large, sensitive ears to stalk its prey—preferably snowshoe hares—and its big paws to walk atop drifts. These and other Interior inhabitants must face temperatures that fall dozens of degrees below zero.

FOLLOWING PAGES: Full-grown antlers mark a male caribou in early autumn—mating season. Female caribou, unique in the deer family, develop antlers too, although much smaller ones.

Wolves, once reviled as voracious demons, now earn praise for culling
weak prey. Reality lies somewhere in between for these opportunistic animals.
Wildlife managers debate how—and if—to balance wolves and prey species.

*"T*he diversity underfoot can be like a tropical rain forest
a few inches tall," says botanist Gary Laursen. Even a square
inch of tundra can host a dozen species of moss. Such variety
is the only spice of winter life for many Alaskan animals.
Dogwood and bearberry (left) redden the White Mountains,
while in Denali a single mountain harebell (below)
pokes through a blanket of large, fuzzy coltsfoot leaves.

CHARLES MAUZY (ABOVE); MIKE O'CONNOR (OPPOSITE)

Camouflage and camaraderie see ptarmigan (bottom) through winter. Barely distinguishable from snowballs, they rest and feed in huge flocks. Thus they elude the wolverine (right), a creature so rapacious that its scientific name means "glutton." In spring, the birds will shed both feathers and friends. Brown-hued, breeding ptarmigan cocks fiercely defend their territories.

FOLLOWING PAGES: "The High One"—Denali in an Athapaskan tongue, Mount McKinley in official nomenclature—towers over late-summer pond lilies.

CRAIG BRANDT
LEN RUE, JR.

GARY SCHULTZ (BELOW). FOLLOWING PAGES: LARRY ULRICH / DRK PHOTO

LON E. LAUBER; FOLLOWING PAGES: KENNAN WARD

A sea otter floats lazily on its back, preparing to feast on a pink salmon thrown to it from a passing fishing boat off the Aleutian Islands.

FOLLOWING PAGES: A brown bear and her cubs take salmon near the coast. In July, browns work these streams in groups as large as 60.

RANGE & GULF:
Otters, Bears, and Moose

God had a field day when He made Alaska's Gulf coast. I mean, He had fun. For starters He fenced it in with North America's tallest mountains, the Alaska Range. He paved one area, the Chugach, with slow-moving scenery: glaciers and icefields in vast, bewildering array. He spattered Katmai, on the Alaska Peninsula, with fumaroles and salmon-rich lakes, rimming some shores with rocks that float. He carved Prince William Sound into an idyllic filigree of countless inlets and steep, forested islands. He endowed the Kenai Peninsula with such a mix of meadows, peaks, glaciers, and other topographic delights that man would later dub the area "Alaska in miniature." And then, just offshore from the Kenai, He *really* indulged Himself: He created Kodiak.

Part emerald isle and part little Switzerland, starburst-shaped Kodiak Island is both lush and alpine. Its size, some 3,800 square miles, ranks it as a mere flake of the Great Land. Still, it is the state's largest island, as well as the most varied. A deeply indented coastline, parts of it dark with spruce, rises boldly from the shadow-blue Gulf of Alaska. Knobby mountains alternate with green hanging valleys, fjordlike inlets, black gravel beaches, and finger lakes that teem with six varieties of salmon. All is fog-drenched and dark and inviting, scored by game trails, countless waterfalls, and streams so crystalline you can count the pebbles on the bottom. The air is brisk and invigoratingly marine even in midsummer, a welcome change from the oppressive heat and insatiable mosquitoes of Fairbanks and the interior.

Kodiak's human history has been long and rich, including a stint as the capital of Russian America. Its current population is about 15,000. Yet the bulk of this island remains roadless and almost defiantly wild, a lush and moody northern Eden where the spectacular is commonplace. But then, what else would you expect from the land of the legendary bear?

"Kodiak," you see, refers not only to an island (and a town and an archipelago), but also to a resident: the world's largest land carnivore. Kodiak bears—the local version of brown or grizzly bears—have a reputation for being bigger and more impressive than those of other regions, and their presence has made this island a favorite of hunters and other wildlife enthusiasts.

"They're trophy bears," declares Vic Barnes, research biologist at the Kodiak National Wildlife Refuge, which occupies two-thirds of the island. "There's no question that a lot of Alaska's trophy bears come from Kodiak."

Ranging up to ten feet tall and 1,500 pounds, they are notable also for their numbers; Alaska's Department of Fish and Game currently estimates that the Kodiak archipelago harbors 2,500 to 3,000 bears, perhaps a tenth of the state's brown/grizzly population. This despite unregulated hunting earlier in this century, and cattle operations that continue even now.

Bears, of course, have been one of the most revered, feared, maligned, misunderstood—and humanlike—of all earth's creatures. Inuit had their bear-god Nanuq. Haida Indians deemed the brown bear a mother-goddess, while Shasta Indians believed that Great Spirit made Bear stronger and cleverer than all other animals, so strong that even his creator fled to a mountaintop for safety. Many Plains tribes considered the grizzly so sacred that although they prized its claws as emblems of great courage, few individuals would dare tan—or even touch—its hide. It was seen as another form of the human animal, a powerful and dark but not necessarily sinister brother to man. No doubt its habit of rearing up on two legs encouraged this sense of brotherhood. So did its possession of personality; bears are as individualistic, as unpredictable, and as perplexing, as people.

Even their taxonomy is confusing. There are black bears *(Ursus americanus)* and brown bears *(Ursus arctos),* a distinction having little to do with color: Both species can vary from straw-blond through dark chocolate to jet. Both also range the bulk of the state. Common usage in Alaska holds that inland brown bears, those away from the influence of salmon, are "grizzlies," while those of coastal regions are "brown bears," with "Kodiak bears" a specialized case. Taxonomists at first agreed, treating brownies and grizzlies as separate species. But when they found that such bears can (and often do) interbreed, they lumped them together as *Ursus arctos,* northern bear. They also determined that Kodiak's island-isolated bruins had developed unique skeletal traits; they really were bigger, enough to warrant their own subspecies classification. And so bears of this archipelago now are dubbed *Ursus arctos middendorffi,* while all other coastal "browns" and inland "grizzlies" are termed *U. a. horribilis.*

Kodiak's bears, says Vic Barnes, deserve their special status. "They're big. About the only others that compare, sizewise, are those of the Alaska Peninsula. And these occur in high densities, they're very visible."

I had to agree about their visibility: I happened to run into one almost as soon as I arrived at Kodiak. Were its eyes really that small, I wondered? Or was it just that the rest of it was so big? The five-gallon head atop the 40-inch neck. The seven-foot height as it stood on hindlegs more massive than most Alaskan trees. The awesome reach of forelimbs extended slightly ahead, like a sleepwalker's arms, except that curved, five-inch-long razors tipped each digit. Then there was the sagging midriff, at least five feet around; a belly like that needs a whole lot of fodder to stay full and happy.

This was the animal I'd come to see, though I hadn't expected to find it quite so soon, in a glass case inside the Kodiak airport. Stuffed animals, I would find, adorn many Alaskan ports of call; it's a way towns can show off not only local wonders of nature but also local taxidermy skills.

The next day, I joined Vic at Karluk Lake, a region of pristine peaks, glacial valleys, rivers, forests, and lakes that he calls "one of the finest—if not *the* finest—brown bear habitats in the world." From a refuge field station here, he and state bear biologist Roger Smith were making daily forays to the remote and relatively unstudied Aliulik Peninsula that forms Kodiak Island's southeastern spur. It was late June, and they were on the prowl for bears.

Not just any bears, mind you—they most wanted adult sows. They'd been doing long-term bear studies, and needed to include females in their data. Another factor was that—since cubs stay with mothers as long as three years—collaring females can be an efficient way to monitor two generations at once. The only hitch was that, this time of year, it's hard enough to tell boars from sows; distinguishing receptive females from nonbreeding ones is well-nigh impossible. About the only way to be sure, Vic explained, is to happen upon them while they're mating. This did not seem to me to be an especially effective prescription for long life.

To deal with such risks, Vic and Roger had devised a sort of aerial hop-scotch, using both a fixed-wing spotter plane and a chase helicopter to locate, pursue, and dart selected bears from the air with a tranquilizer gun. Whenever the biologists descended to record a downed bear's vital statistics and attach a radio collar, the chopper pilot could go back up to track nearby bears, heading them off if they got too close. The plane, meanwhile, would search for the next one to dart. Everyone kept in touch by radio.

It sounded straightforward, and Aliulik's sweeping scapes were mostly tundra and muskeg, with no trees and seemingly few hiding spots. But bears have a knack for disappearing into the slightest alder clump or tussock ridge. Butch Patterson—flying the fixed-wing SuperCub—is a long time airborne, while Vic, Roger, and I sit in the grounded chopper with pilot Herb Downs, watching Sitka black-tailed deer graze, scatter, and regroup. A lone bald eagle wheels and flaps over a nearby lake, searching for a quick fish dinner. Most of the deer are females, heavy with fawns about to drop. Like mountain goats and Roosevelt elk (on nearby Afognak Island), Kodiak's deer were introduced from mainland stocks; all three imports have done well.

Finally the long-silent radio crackles. It's Butch: "We got a single, kind of blond-colored, over on that creek where we were yesterday."

The chopper lifts off, everyone scanning the sky for Butch while he radios us a running account of the bear's whereabouts. Soon Herb has it in sight. He touches down a safe distance away to disgorge unnecessary weight—that is, Roger and me. Vic, the darter this time around, stays on board as Herb returns to the air and closes in on the quarry, which breaks into a lumbering run. Herb plays position, nudging the bear left or right with his chopper as a cowboy might guide a panicky steer.

Suddenly the bear swings wide and veers uphill, toward Roger and me. Its bulky yet fluid gait is deceptively fast as it lopes effortlessly over terrain that would slow us to a crawl: low-growing alder tangles, soggy muskeg, grassy tussocks. Herb's attempts to turn it are ignored. It seems less an animal than a runaway locomotive.

"Stay back, stay back," Roger cautions as I edge slightly forward. Stay back where, I wonder? No way we can outrun this bear, and there aren't any trees to climb. We're not even sure Vic scored a hit.

Butch is, however. He's been circling high above, and now his radio voice coos: "C'mon sweetheart, go down. Go down right there. Okay, she's losing it in the hindquarters."

Finally, the pulsing muscles slow; the bear totters into a thicket. Herb pulls back, waiting for the drug to take full effect, then drops Vic at the site and zips back to pick us up. By the time we arrive, Vic has the dart out. He and Roger declare it a prize female in prime shape, perhaps 20 years old and 500 pounds. The lightly snoring head *is* huge. But this can't be the same body that was thundering toward me seconds ago; it's so small, like a deflated balloon. Bears always are biggest when they're coming your way.

Roger and Vic, still marveling at the sow's great condition, attach ear tags and tattoo identifying numbers on her groin and inside her lip. They draw blood samples and a vestigial premolar (to establish her age more accurately), inject penicillin (to offset possible infection caused by today's procedures), and finally bolt a big white plastic radio collar about her neck. Now she looks not only small but captive, the tags and wide collar recalling images of a circus bear—or a Gary Larson cartoon. Suddenly the eyes blink open; a moany growl escapes her lips. The eyes see us, the ears hear, the sensitive, quivering nose definitely smells us. Her drug-induced helplessness will last only another 20 minutes or so; then she will be up and away.

Bears are survivors, and they routinely give—and take—far worse punishment from each other than we have doled out today. Still, Vic is quick to acknowledge that such field operations put animals at risk.

"It's a legitimate concern. I won't deny it's a lot of fun being here. But we're not doing this just to wrassle with bears. Once you locate an animal, chase it down and subject it to this kind of stress—and there's no other way to put it—you have an obligation to that animal and the species to follow through and do the hard work. This—the darting and collaring—is really the easy part. The hard part is maintaining your tracking schedule after the collars are on, going out and keeping track of animals and taking down information and writing it up. It's a grind."

He and Roger, he feels, are "really conservative. Our highest priority is the safety of the crew. But the next highest priority is the safety of the bear. It's devastating when you kill an animal. We've killed a couple. You hate it. And you do everything you can to avoid it."

"But," I asked, "why so many tattoos? You gave some of those bears three or four—plus the two ear tags—just to identify them. Is all that really necessary?"

"The short answer," said Roger, "is 'yes.' Every tattoo doesn't end up being legible. As an animal ages it gets a lot more pigmentation; the skin gets to be darn-near black. In fact, the oldest bear on record—35 years—was identified by ear tags. You couldn't see the tattoos."

Aging bears from annular rings on their teeth, he admits, "is not all science; there's a fair bit of art in interpreting ages. But it's 80 or 90 percent accurate, on younger animals. It's worth doing."

Vic agrees: "The more accurate ages we have, the better. It's a vestigial tooth; it's not functional. Sure, it's traumatic to be chased, it's stressful to have a tooth pulled. Probably one of the biggest things is that dart hitting them; it gives them a big bruise. But it's unavoidable. You know, these animals are extremely tough, extremely resilient—and we have no evidence that our capture operations have a lasting, negative influence. We know there's stress, but we try to minimize it."

Many wildlife lovers see the collars as a detriment; they detract visually, making the bear look less than wild, and they chafe the skin.

Indeed, they are snug—especially on males. Boars have heads that— huge as they are—are smaller than their necks. How can you hope to keep a collar on them, if it's not tight? But, says Roger, "There's just no method we've found for putting a radio on a bear that's better than putting it around his neck. We've never had a bear die from a collar being too tight. It just doesn't happen. I've seen some *horrible* natural wounds that bears live with. A collar is a minor inconvenience."

Not to hunters, who want a pelt without the neck hair worn off, and not to guides who want happy clients. Hunting is a small but important part of the Kodiak economy, and even part of the research scene; state biologists record the sex, skull size, and approximate age of each bear that is taken. Of course, if the bear had a say in the matter, it might prefer a collar to a bullet and a distant observer with field glasses to either.

In the past, wildlife biologists such as Adolph Murie assumed a more purely observational, low-technology stance. Things are different today.

"Those guys did some outstanding work," says Vic. "But there are lots of things they couldn't do, like figure mortality rates, or learn how bears move when they wean. In the field, you only see what's easy to see." Managing whole populations of bear or other wildlife, he adds, demands statistically significant numbers: information on an entire group. Watching single bears and dens, as Murie and others did, simply doesn't yield that sort of data.

With radios, says Roger, "We're able to follow the same animals year after year, and *know* the age of the cubs. Before, they could only guess."

So it is that these days, among wildlife researchers, radiotelemetry is hot. There are radioed bears on Kodiak, radioed moose roaming the former National Moose Range (now a national wildlife refuge) on the Kenai Peninsula. There also are radioed sea otters swimming and diving and feeding in Prince William Sound, part of studies trying to determine impacts of the 1989 *Exxon Valdez* oil spill, the nation's worst. Because otters are so agile and active, and because their fur loses its insulative qualities when compressed, otter biologists forgo collars or harnesses and instead implant radios surgically. Critics, says Roger, will always exist.

"The question is, can you see the forest for the trees? Do we want to learn about what's going to happen, or do we not? Do we want to rely on anecdotal type stuff, just fly out and look around, or do we want to have good, solid data to make our management decisions? Right now, there's no substitute for capturing animals, handling them, and putting radios on them. It's the best piece of technology that's been developed. Particularly when you're dealing with vast areas and the airplane is the only way you can go."

"The anomaly," Vic adds, "is that we work so hard to save these bears—and then we allow 150 of them to be killed by hunters every year. That's kind of a contradiction." An avid hunter of other species, Vic has no desire to shoot bears himself. But hunting plays a role in management, and getting a close estimate of the bear population is essential for setting the hunters' quota.

Relatively few bear hunters visit the Aliulik Peninsula, because of its fickle weather and dearth of landing spots for floatplanes, the island's chief transportation. Also, there is a feeling that the barren, tussocky, potholed terrain makes inferior bear habitat. But in just a few days here, we see dozens of animals. Roger decides that there could easily be 200 of them—double an earlier estimate—and starts planning for intensive surveys next year.

It's often said that in the Brooks Range and much of the interior, a lone grizzly needs 100 or even 200 square miles to survive. Here, the minimum area seems less than a mile. Of course, Aliulik is much more temperate than the far north. But the peninsula has no salmon runs until August. Its deer, while plentiful, are far too fleet for bears to catch in such wide-open country. How could so many bears be in such great shape so early, having left their dens only recently? Sows, which give birth to cubs in midwinter and nurse them all through the denning period without eating, should have been especially skinny. But they weren't. What were they feeding on?

"Bears are not necessarily predators," said Vic, adding that he and Roger also had been initially surprised by Aliulik's high bear density. "I think they've got a little different feeding ecology here than on the rest of the island. The climate's milder—these animals may come out of their dens earlier, and go in later. They may not require as much fat or expend as much in the wintertime. But they clearly have a lot of food. They orient toward these 'collector beaches' that happen to gather a lot of ocean debris."

"All kinds of stuff washes up there," said Roger. "Dead sea lions, sea otters, seals, whales, seabirds, fish. It's a tremendous carrion source. Also, it's got huge offshore kelp beds, which are full of life. You get a lot of kelp breaking loose and coming in."

The kelp, Vic added, "is just full of 'beach fleas'"—tiny but prolific arthropods, a good protein source. "Bears just constantly eat. I'm sure these guys get more seals and sea lions, compared to most other bears. They also get dead deer left from winter, and seabirds and eggs. It's pretty obvious just from their distribution that, in early summer, they're getting almost all their food within a half or even a quarter-mile of the beach."

Come August, he added, "Aliulik has just incredibly strong runs of pink salmon. You'll see thirty and forty bears along the streams, probably putting on two or three pounds a day, each. It's a short burst, but when it's there the bears really go for it. In summer they need to gain 25 or 30 percent of their body weight in fat, and quality-wise, fish are real important."

But hold it—aren't bears loners? Solitary monarchs of the wilderness?

Says Roger, "They're solitary in the Interior, where they aren't very dense. It's not that they're solitary animals socially, it just takes a lot of land to keep one of them alive. But anywhere you've got a concentrated food source—like these beaches here—those rules are all suspended."

"Yeah," agrees Vic. "You find sows within a couple hundred yards of each other, all doing the same things. They get along. A lot of them may even be related, just good buddies. I've seen groups of three and four and five great big boars late in the fall, all within a couple of acres. That's not very unsociable. They're all here because there's a food source, and they've worked out a pecking order."

He adds, "It's fine to talk about 'the Kodiak bear,' its life and habits. But there're a lot of contrasts, even on this small archipelago. Right now you've got bears on Dog Salmon Creek eating salmon. You've got bears over here eating whatever they find on the beach. And you've got bears grazing, up in the alpine. There're different strategies, different ways bears make their living between the south and north and Aliulik. There're a lot of differences in the foods they eat, how they behave, where they den, their travels."

To say nothing of differences in personality.

"They're not herd animals," says Roger. "With bears, you see a lot more individualism, just like with humans."

Across Shelikof Strait from Kodiak, on the Alaska Peninsula, streamside parades of brown bears seasonally draw human crowds to Katmai National Park's Brooks Camp. Both it and the nearby McNeil River State Game Sanctuary are wonderful places to see large numbers of bears in relatively little space; you walk to observation areas at river's edge. At Brooks Camp there's a good chance you'll see Diver—at twenty-something a relatively old boar, named for his unusual habit of porpoising slowly through the shallows in pursuit of fish. Perhaps you'll also be entertained—as I was—by three two-and-a-half-year-old cubs, recently chucked out of childhood by their mom, and making dawn patrols along the lakeshore. They romped in the water and on the beach, rising up on rear legs to wrestle and buffet and nuzzle each other. Then they broke clinches and toddled off, one cub's paw draped on another's shoulder, the trio looking like school buddies headed home after a hard-fought ballgame. Minutes later, they were back roughhousing, then enjoying a quick, cooling-off dip. One youngster lay on its back and rocked side to side, all four paws in the air. "Like cats on catnip," commented a park ranger.

McNeil River and Brooks both are places where animals come and go at will while people are controlled. Some control is needed. Because while bears and humans may be brothers in myth, historically we've gotten along about as well as Cain and Abel, and the bears haven't fared well. Now, we've set aside these preserves—in part for the animals but also because we want to see them up close. The bears of summer are nonstop food processors, spending all their time feeding and napping, bulking up for winter. They come to McNeil and Katmai for salmon, not to see or be seen. Usually they avoid conflict, even when something gets between them and their food. But sometimes the intruder—human or otherwise—is interpreted as a threat and attacked. Even the playful youngsters can be inadvertently dangerous. They outweigh us by at least a hundred pounds, and don't know their strength—or what humans are all about. Many humans here know even less about bears; they often set aside their healthy fear of the species because they seem calm or even friendly, almost tame.

But they are not. An overzealous photographer unknowingly intrudes on a bear's private space; the bear turns and defends itself—an act humans see as attack. Or a flyfisherman finally hooks a trophy salmon—only to see a bruin approach, curious at the fish's splashings. Unwilling to surrender his prize so soon, he foolishly plays the salmon, drawing the bear closer. At last he has to slash his line and flee. Even if he loses nothing more than the fish, the episode is not harmless. For the bear has learned today to link the presence of its two-legged brother with a gift of salmon. Next time it spots a fisherman, it may approach more aggressively, expecting that reward. Another "incident" results.

Managing bear hunters is easy, or relatively so; just close a season or reduce a bag limit. Managing nonhunters is much more difficult. For one thing, they're more plentiful. And their effect can be more lingering, because as wild animals become habituated to people, they may lose their fear of man.

McNeil River takes the lottery approach, limiting total visitation to 295 people in an 80-day season. It's fine if you win a slot, but some Alaskans say they've tried for seven or eight years without success—while a few lucky ones have visited more than once.

Katmai's Brooks Camp is more liberal, allowing only 120 overnighters at one time. It lays down rules, both for men and beasts. On arrival, park visitors receive guidelines on how to behave around bears and minimum distances to keep between themselves and the animals. The bears roam free except for campsites and other human-used areas; rangers punish intrusions by firing explosive "cracker" shells and rubber bullets, hoping to "educate" wayward bears before they become hardcore "problem bears."

Both Brooks and McNeil seek to maintain an artificial situation—critics say they're disasters waiting to happen—because repeated exposure to people only emboldens bears. While the animals quickly establish a pecking order among themselves, they aren't allowed to do so with humans. Still, some keep trying. My last morning at Brooks, in fact, a rogue bear blew through the campground and shredded two tents—one just a few feet from mine. There was no food inside, no provocation. Luckily, no one was hurt. But the incident points up Katmai's—and McNeil's—enduring dilemma. Is it really possible to fully protect bears *and* people? When dustups occur, human safety obviously gets top priority; "problem" bears ultimately get translocated or shot.

In short, the "bear problem" is just one aspect of the more general "parks problem": We set aside certain lands because we want to save them, but also because we want to use them. As human traffic increases, we imperil those very features that park designation was supposed to preserve for all time. Today, Alaska's brown bears have become such a tourist magnet—in large part because of the species' virtual extermination in the lower 48—that demand for bear-watching areas well exceeds supply. In 1992, such pressures encouraged creation of a new observation area on Kodiak, near the south end of Karluk Lake.

Native landholders control some 300,000 acres of the island, including large tracts of Karluk, and they are eager for a share of tourist dollars. Development—one of the questions ANILCA and ANCSA were supposed to answer 20 years ago but really just set aside—again looms.

Vic Barnes is pensive on the subject. "Bringing in hordes of people, on top of a high density of bears. I don't think anyone would suggest that's going to wipe out the bear population. But it *will* detract from the situation as we know it today. The Kodiak bear is a special animal. Everybody—when they think about bears, they think about *Kodiak* bears. We don't want to save a few of them, we want the situation to stay the way it is right now."

Roger Smith, equally concerned, says, "I'm not real optimistic that we're going to solve the problem of bears coming into conflict with people in cabins and fishing sites and lodges. It's so hard to convince people that they are the ones creating a hazard."

FOLLOWING PAGES: Brown bears shake off after a swim. Fine swimmers, browns will enter the water to fish, to drink, to cool off, or just for a romp.

Coastal browns emerge from their dens in March, April, or May, often with snow still on the ground. At right, a youngster finds relief on the rough bark of a favored "bear tree," partially stripped by years of scratching. Adults (below) nuzzle to show mutual acceptance during courtship and mating, which takes place between May and July. By August the bears are eating as much as 90 pounds of food a day to prepare for their winter sleep. Cubs, usually twins, are born in the den in January or February; they stay with their mother for two or three years. She teaches them to fish, forage, hunt, and defend themselves. A playful brown (left) yawns mightily and stretches in the summer sun at Denali National Park.

A bull moose in Denali National Park glowers, head down, ready to charge. A mature bull may weigh as much as 1,800 pounds, with antlers six feet from tip to tip. Size counts during mating season, when the males joust in shoving matches, antlers clashing. The winner takes the female. Below, a cow nuzzles her new calf while it noses fresh spring shoots.

KENNAN WARD; CRAIG BRANDT (OPPOSITE)

JIM BRANDENBURG; ROBERT LANKINEN / THE WILDLIFE COLLECTION (ABOVE)

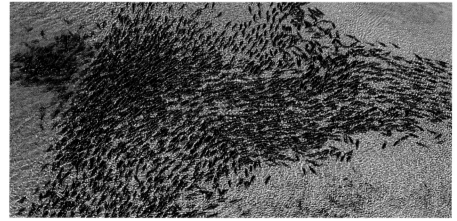

Sockeye salmon (left) congregate in Lake Clark before they swim up feeder streams to spawn. Worn out by their upstream journey, the spent salmon will fall easy prey to river otters, which feast on whatever fish and shellfish are most abundant and easy to catch. A river otter can travel underwater for hundreds of yards before surfacing for air. These graceful swimmers, smaller and more streamlined than sea otters, are swift enough to catch a trout in open water. Extremely playful, they can spend hours chasing each other, wrestling, diving for rocks, and sliding down muddy riverbanks.

Gum eraser lichens, moss, and Sitka alder thrive in the cool, misty summers along the coast of Kenai Fjords National Park. These plants are the first to colonize bare rock scoured by glaciers. On an inland meadow, a small Apollo butterfly sips nectar from a forget-me-not. The eggs of this species, laid in late summer, will hatch next year.

DAVID MUENCH; FRED HIRSCHMANN (LEFT)

*B*ald eagles battle over salmon carcasses at the Alaska Chilkat Bald Eagle Preser

which protects the world's largest concentration of these birds.

BOB HALLINEN / ALASKA STOCK IMAGES; RON SANFORD (ABOVE)

*P*ortage Glacier feeds ice and meltwater to pristine Portage Lake (above). Sixty miles eastward, in Prince William Sound, harbor seals relax on a floe calved by Columbia Glacier. Ice-filled waters often give seals a refuge from killer whales, their major predators. Local populations of sea mammals and birds have declined since the Exxon Valdez oil spill in the sound in 1989. Many scientists believe that oil-contaminated mussels and fishes are poisoning the sound's entire food chain.

A killer whale, or orca, breaches in Kachemak Bay, near the Kenai range. Highly intelligent and sociable, orcas travel in family pods of as many as 50 members that hunt, rest, and play together. They live 40 years or more, growing as long as 25 feet and weighing as much as 6 tons. Orcas feed on fish, dolphins, seals, sea lions, and other whales—and have no enemies but humans.

FOLLOWING PAGES: A sea otter hugs her pup as they nap in a bed of kelp. Mother and young are inseparable for the first year.

RICHARD JOHNSON / ALASKA STOCK IMAGES.
FOLLOWING PAGES: DANIEL J. COX

DOUG PERRINE / DRK PHOTO. FOLLOWING PAGES: JOHN HYDE / ALASKA STOCK IMAGES

Endangered acrobats, humpback whales summer along Pacific coasts. Once coveted—and easy—prey for whalers, they now lure enthusiastic wildlife watchers.

FOLLOWING PAGES: Summertime, and the feeding is easy.... For this humpback in Chatham Strait, an arc through a school of herring yields a feast.

PANHANDLE:
Ancient Forest, Deer, and Whales

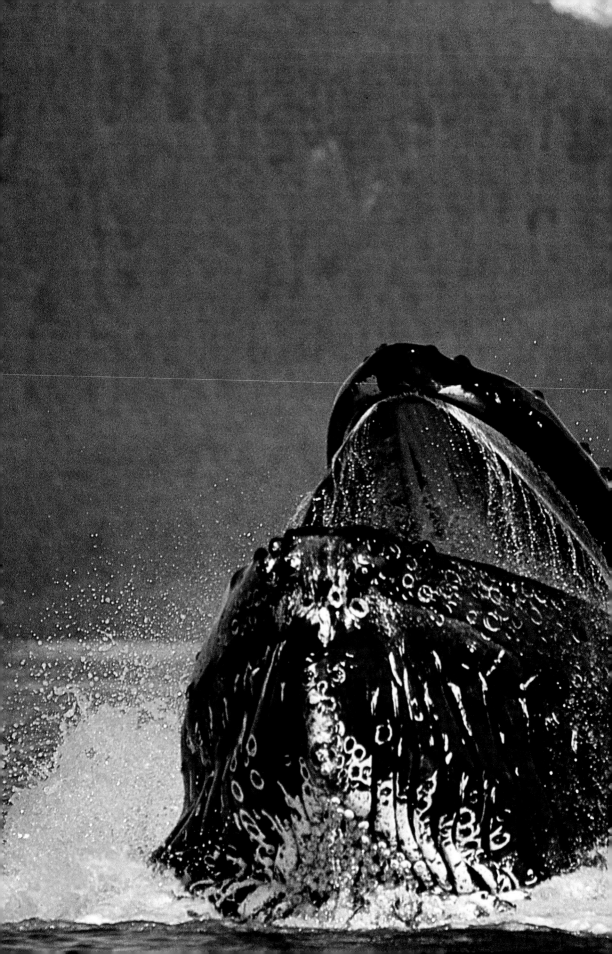

"This isn't part of Alaska," bear researcher LaVern Beier says with a straight face, though the region he refers to falls squarely within state lines. Known variously as "the Panhandle," "Southeast," even "the other Alaska," it's been his home for the past 23 years. "Alaska," he explains, "is igloos and polar bears—that's what a lot of folks think. They don't think of it as rain forest. But *that's* what Southeast is all about. I think it's some of the most spectacular country in the state. Even though it's been logged for nearly 40 years. It's totally different from the Interior."

Indeed it is. Hemmed between the rugged Coast Mountains and the Pacific Ocean, Alaska's Panhandle stands in isolation, a region ruled by water: a land of fjords and glaciers and twisting streams, of limpid tarns and luxuriant muskeg, where annual rainfall often exceeds a hundred inches. Most of all, it is a realm of trees and wildlife.

This is temperate rain forest, one of the few still largely intact. The climate is so wet and cool that lightning-caused fires are all but nonexistent, so deadfalls and underbrush clutter the ground. Entire communities of tiny plants beard tree limbs and trunks, both living and dead. As old giants fall, they rip holes in the canopy, allowing sunlight to reach the forest floor and stimulate new growth. Although such 300- to 500-year-old monarchs are unusual, the forest itself is ancient and extremely stable, basically unchanged since glaciers beat their last retreat some 10,000 years ago. Western hemlock and Sitka spruce predominate. Southeast has a lot of rock, ice, and muskeg as well as rain forest, and its trees run the gamut from giant "pumpkin spruce" five or six feet across to some rather scrawny and stunted mountain hemlocks—often within a single drainage.

"It's a messy forest," says Matt Kirchoff, a deer research biologist with the state's Department of Fish and Game. "It's overgrown and brushy, not parklike at all. But hike it from coast to mountaintop, and you go through many completely different types of habitat. The structure of the forest changes dramatically. So does its value to different wildlife."

About 300 species of animals roam Southeast's forests, among them black and brown bears, wolves and moose, Sitka black-tailed deer, various furbearers, raptors, also voles and mice and other woodland creatures. Brown bear densities rank among the world's highest. An estimated 12,000 to 15,000 bald eagles nest here, in greater density than anywhere else. Ravens, woodpeckers, and waterfowl abound. Even mountain goats, associated more often with steep crags, turn to the forest for food as well as for winter shelter.

In 1907, President Theodore Roosevelt, fighting the destructive logging practices of his day, proclaimed 21 new national forests—among them, the Tongass. Today it boasts 17 million acres; it's by far the nation's largest, bigger than West Virginia. Include two spacious national monuments administered by the Forest Service, and you have a single agency overseeing some 85 percent of the Panhandle. So, LaVern Beier is right to say Southeast isn't Alaska: it's the Tongass, and Tongass *is* Southeast.

Of all the forest's varied habitats, says Matt Kirchoff, the one most important to wildlife is a relatively rare type known as the "high-volume old growth." Simply put, it's where the biggest trees and highest canopies occur, usually along drainages and more gradual slopes.

"It's a really critical biological area," agrees John Sisk, formerly the executive director of the Southeast Alaska Conservation Council, a coalition of grassroots environmental groups. "It includes a lot of salmon streams and critical winter habitat for deer. It's where everything happens."

Plentiful berry patches and salmon runs make the high-volume forest a magnet for bears both black and brown. Bald eagles prefer its tall trees for nesting sites and overviews of fishing areas. Sitka black-tailed deer find both forage and shelter under its giant canopy, which deflects winter's formidable snows. Marten—prized by furriers as "American sable"—also seek high-volume areas. They prey on small animals, staking out extensive territories, and sometimes make their dens high in the canopy.

Yet another species prefers the high-volume old growth to other forest types: man. Sport hunters, fishermen, and wildlife watchers come for the animal life. Others revel in the unique and humbling scenic appeal of these forests primeval. And then, of course, there are the timber interests, drawn by the giant trees that yield the most and highest-quality wood.

National forests are not tree sanctuaries but repositories of public resources to be managed on a long-term, sustained-yield basis. This has been the mission of the U.S. Forest Service, which has administered the Tongass and all other national forests, in this century. While it does not cut or mill trees, it sells stands to logging companies and builds roads to reach those stands. Its mandate is one of "multiple use"—that is, devoting portions of forest to recreation and conservation as well as to commercial timber production—and this often means multiple conflict and controversy. But it focuses primarily on building roads and harvesting trees. This has been especially true in the Tongass.

In addition to scenic and esthetic concerns, there are biological ones. Scalp the forest too close to a stream and erosion muddies the water; sunlight pours down on the creek, raising its temperature and affecting fish; without trees to fall into the stream and create natural pools, salmon and trout have fewer places to rest. Creeks become faster-flowing, more direct—and more biologically impoverished.

Dramatic inland changes also may result. Studies show that bears avoid cutover streams even when salmon runs continue. Sitka black-tailed deer will roam recent clear-cuts for forage, but in a few years those cuts close in with brush, and the deer go elsewhere.

Already, at least 400,000 acres of forest—mostly high-volume—have been clear-cut since 1954, and the Forest Service has declared another 1.5 to 1.9 million acres "suitable for harvest" over the next 100 years. The total area, roughly 2.3 million acres, may sound modest as against the 17 million acres in the Tongass. But only 60 percent of Southeast—10 million acres—is forested, and less than 60 percent of that is classified as commercial timber: that is, capable of yielding at least 8,000 board feet per acre, the lowest quantity worth cutting.

"That's a pretty scrubby bottom limit," says Matt. "You're talking about very gnarly, small trees at that stage, commercial in name only. It's the high-volume old growth—more than 30,000 board feet per acre—that's been logged in the past and is the focus of most logging pressure today."

Such stands represent the heart of the forest, the best of the best, both in terms of timber and wildlife habitat. Estimates of the total high-volume forest in the Tongass today range from half a million acres to a million. Depending on what stands are cut, loggers could reduce the high-volume old growth so severely that wildlife populations could plummet. Thus the dilemma of Southeast: It's a 17-million-acre pie, but everyone wants the same slice. Battles over how to use these forests have raged off and on for decades, and won't end soon. At the center of it all lies the Forest Service.

Back in the late 1940s and early '50s, planners decided that southeast Alaska's economic salvation lay with the Tongass. The timber industry, they said, would provide year-round jobs that would free the region from its boom-and-bust cycles. In those years, foresters considered old growth not only renewable but improvable: Clear-cutting it would allow the land to put forth second-growth trees, favored because they were more uniform. Selective thinning would increase the percentage of spruce, a higher-value wood. Man would improve on nature, which had never perfected a tree farm.

Meanwhile, government virtually gave away the store: 50-year contracts—unheard of in the Forest Service before or since, but mandated by Congress—guaranteed logging companies huge yearly cuts and extremely low prices on standing timber. The agency also agreed to pay for thousands of miles of roads, or credit the companies if they built them. And while the Forest Service officially determined the size and location of every clear-cut, in practice the loggers often had their own way. Naturally, they preferred the high-volume stands.

Why should they need the best timber, when their mills produced pulp, not high-value timber products? For one thing, it's more efficient to take the biggest trees. For another, they could make big money by reselling better-grade timber to sawmills—because the price they paid was geared to the low value of pulp, not to the premium prices that top-quality sawlogs fetched on the open market. Over the years this margin widened: In the 1980s, loggers often paid less than one percent of market prices. Whole trees went for the price of cheeseburgers.

Also, provisions of ANILCA created an annual "Tongass Timber Supply Fund" to offset the effects of designating areas as wilderness and to help maintain employment levels. The fund received at least $40 million a year. In some years it got more than $60 million, as road-building costs soared to $250,000 a mile. One government study noted that if the annual timber fund was simply distributed directly to loggers and pulp mill workers, each would get about $36,000 a year—a pay raise for some—and no trees would need to be cut, no roads built, no wildlife habitat disturbed.

"To justify that kind of subsidy," says John Sisk, "usually there's an end result you point to that is something really great for society. But the result of this is a biological wasteland as far as wildlife habitat goes. We're getting something negative in return for the subsidy instead of something positive."

Others said the Forest Service was giving away an irreplaceable national treasure, trading ancient forests—and a lot of money—for dirt roads. Years of complaints and antitrust action culminated in the Tongass Timber Reform

Act of 1990, which ended the annual supply fund and brought stumpage fees closer to market values. Even so, the trees-for-roads swap continued, perpetuating the incentive to log big trees. Claims John, "A spruce log they pay the Forest Service somewhere between $50 and $250 a thousand board feet for, the real pumpkin spruce, they can sell for $2,400 a thousand."

What's "really kind of pathetic," he adds, is that the local pulp mills haven't prospered after all.

He does not advocate a complete end to logging, nor do any wildlife biologists I met. But they all want stronger curbs against "high-grading" the forest—that is, taking the biggest and best stands and leaving the rest.

Wayne Nicolls, public affairs director for the Alaska region of the Forest Service, vehemently denies that high-grading occurs, and even calls the term "an insult and a four-letter word." But numerous field biologists familiar with the Tongass—as well as some Forest Service regulars—insist that high-grading has been a reality here for years.

"High-grading is a real concern to wildlife mangers," maintains Fish and Game biologist Rod Flynn, who studies marten in some actively logged sections of Chichagof Island. "The highest quality, the most productive, the largest trees are being removed at a rapid rate." The Tongass Reform Act prohibited high-grading, but its terms were open to interpretation in the field.

In 1993, however, three groups—the Alaska chapter of the Wildlife Society, the Wilderness Society, and the Sierra Club—brought a test case. They sued the Forest Service, asking a federal judge to postpone a sale of timber at Kelp Bay on Baranof Island. The service's maps of timber types, they said, are so inaccurate that sales based on them are "arbitrary and capricious" and therefore unlawful. Its estimates of high-volume timber at the site were 2 or 3 percent; its field check revealed 50 percent and suggested "an alarming degree of high-grading." Lawyers for the service defended its procedures and suggested that if too much high-volume old growth were cut for one sale, more low-volume timber could be cut in future. All parties agreed that the judge's decision would affect future offerings of timber in the Tongass, whether or not it had the old-growth charm of Kelp Bay.

"Sometimes," says Matt Kirchoff, the deer biologist, "it seems the Forest Service views 'multiple-use' as managing every acre for everyone: a little logging, a little of this and that. Well, in some cases, a little logging isn't compatible with other things. Especially wildlife and recreation. I've always been a strong proponent of dedicating some sites 100 percent to logging—especially second-growth sites. But you absolutely cannot go into every single drainage and take the very best timber out and then, ten years later, go back in and take the very best of what's left."

Yet that is just what's happening in many parts of Tongass, say the biologists, and it's impairing wildlife habitat. The Forest Service takes the view that wildlife can and will make do with less than its ideal habitat. It also contends that removal of old-growth often benefits wildlife, by allowing sunlight to stimulate growth of forage plants.

"That's been one of the assumptions," says Rod. "People say, small rodents are abundant in clear-cuts. When we first started this research, our clear-cut transects did have high numbers of mice and voles. But now they've gone way down—while in old-growth areas they've gone from intermediate numbers to just slightly lower. Old-growth appears to be a more stable environment. Its fluctuations of temperature and humidity and such are less. In clear-cuts, our animal numbers fluctuate more wildly. A few years ago, there were so many voles in some clear-cuts that people were concerned they might damage the tree seedlings. This trip, we haven't counted *any* voles. I don't know what's happened. Boom and bust? Rain? We have no proof."

Proof is a difficult issue for the field biologist. The Forest Service supports Rod's work, helping him to pursue his own research project.

"But," he says, "there's a double standard. The burden of proof is always on researchers to show that there is a negative impact, and what that is. But the flip side is that the timber people assume that there's *no* impact.

"What's closer to the truth is that the old-growth forest is essentially nonrenewable, and essentially lost." Old-growth stands, he explains, "are the product of thousands of years of trees growing and dying, falling down, creating small gaps, growing very slowly on a particular piece of ground. You can't duplicate that structure—in terms of the stand, the trees, wood quality, or the habitat—unless you go through the same long-term events. A single tree may be 250 years old. But it grew up in a stand that was *hundreds* of years old; it will take a lot more than 250 years to replace that."

One of the biggest problems Rod and other biologists face is that Southeast is so cloaked in forest that aerial surveys just don't work. How do you count all the animals and determine population trends? If you can't do that, how do you forecast where the population is headed? Many biologists seek answers through computer models. Established facts—such as habitat preference and logging data—go in, and the computer indicates how a species might respond over time to different variables. Such models, says Matt, suggest that deer could plunge 20 to 40 percent within the decade.

Marten, Rod adds, "show a very high preference, not just for old-growth forests, but for the *higher volume* old growth. They definitely avoid clear-cut areas. But if you have a little patchwork forest, will they still run around between clear-cuts? Or do you reach a point where there's a threshold and suddenly the marten are gone, because the habitat's not concentrated enough? How much forest can you remove and still have marten there? That's a question that really has not been answered."

Clear-cutting's effects on wildlife are not always obvious early on. Weather and the ability of species to adapt to lesser environments can mask the biological impacts of logging for years. For example, heavily logged Prince of Wales Island, at the southern and most productive end of the Panhandle, has lost much of its high-volume old growth. As yet, no dramatic declines in wildlife have been detected. But biologists point out that recent winters have been mild. Hit a streak of snowier-than-normal winters, however, and the island's lack of cover may cause catastrophic die-offs of deer.

In the lower 48, deer have flourished greatly in second-growth woodland. That might not prove true in Alaska, wrote a wildlife biologist for the Forest Service in 1981. "Even in summer," warned Olof C. Wallmo, the early-stage vegetation is "too dense to be used by deer," and later stages "have impoverished understories that are poor deer habitat at best."

Also at issue is fragmentation. In nature, large wildlife populations spread over large habitats usually survive best. But nature split Southeast into a thousand islands and numerous isolated wildlife populations, and now logging has fragmented it even more. Populations are growing smaller and more vulnerable. Roads, in fact, present more of a hazard for some species than do the actual clear-cuts. On the northeast portion of Chichagof Island, hunters' take of bears doubled in 1980, following a spate of roading; recently it more than tripled, and Fish and Game closed the hunt. Since many more roads are planned for northeast Chichagof, biologists fear the viability of its local bear population is in question.

Many compare southeast Alaska today to the Pacific Northwest of 80 or 100 years ago; most forest remains uncut, but much has been targeted by industry. Keep clear-cutting the old growth and eventually you will threaten some creature's survival. The Endangered Species Act will kick in—as it did a few years ago in the Pacific Northwest, where the spotted owl now holds the entire timber industry at bay. Giving loggers basically a free hand until such a crisis occurs, say the biologists, is no way to manage industry or wildlife. You simply reel from one wildlife crisis to another.

This week it's the spotted owl. Next, the snail darter. Or maybe... marten. While threatened species often can be brought back from the brink, it's very expensive to do so, and invoking the Endangered Species Act promises to convulse both logging and hunting interests. It makes more economic and ecological sense, say the biologists, to avoid creating such crises in the first place, and instead to manage the ecosystem as a whole. And in 1994 a new chief, Jack Ward Thomas, declared that the service should adopt such an approach, to sustain "both the economy and the environment."

Some Forest Service employees admit their agency has been reluctant to act on biologists' warnings. But they point out that the agency has instituted minimum buffer zones of standing forest along streams and seacoast. Most clear-cuts, they add, don't exceed 100 acres.

Until 1990, however, privately owned lands carried no such restrictions. Some holdings on Chichagof Island display hills scalped clean from peak to waterline. Entire slopes stand totally bare. Even now the forest is cast into the sea, towed to Hoonah, and there loaded onto Japanese freighters as raw logs and shipped off.

Ironically, the owners of these lands belong to a group that society has long considered an ecological paragon: the American Indian. These are thoroughly corporate Indians, stockholders in Sealaska, which is the regional Native corporation.

ANCSA, the Alaska Native Claims Settlement Act of 1971, called for the creation of such corporations and endowed them with millions of acres chosen by Natives from nearby federal lands. Naturally, they picked the best acreages available. Sealaska, one of the richer Native corporations, is currently clear-cutting large tracts of its 330,000 acres.

Thus the land suffers. And while it may have different owners, it is viewed—and to that extent shared—by all.

LaVern Beier, tagging bears on Chichagof, gestures at the surrounding landscape and says, "Anywhere else, this would be a national park. Where else on the planet can you see this kind of country, that's not mucked up? But nowadays, more and more, I go back to some quiet, wild, pristine bay or cove where I anchored my boat and trapped or fished or camped, and there's logging trucks and chain saws running, and this whole mountainside with no trees on it anymore. It really tears me up.

"You know, if we lived to be 400 years old rather than 70, we might have more reverence for the land and its resources. They're kind of disposable to us mortals, because we don't live long enough. If we knew we had to live with our mistakes for 400 years of our lives, our attitudes might be different."

Bush pilot Lynn Bennett, bound for Chichagof Island, passes over scattered clear-cuts in the Tongass, then nears Sealaska's ravaged hills.

"They're gutting one of the best salmon and brown bear streams left in the area. Just gutting it," Lynn fumes. As a pilot, he sees more of the Southeast than most. While no one really likes clear-cuts, Lynn used to accept them as economic necessity.

Early on, his flying business prospered from timber-industry bookings. He agreed when his clients criticized "tree-huggers" as extremists unreasonably opposed to progress and development. "To me, 'environmentalist' used to be a four-letter word," he says today. "Now, I guess I'm slipping more and more toward being one, every time I see a few more clear-cuts. I've just been driven to it by seeing some of the things that are going on here.

"About four years ago, I flew for a logging camp up on Chilkat Peninsula, made some money off it. Now, I fly 300 people a day to Gustavus to see Glacier Bay National Park and the beautiful scenery enroute. Guess what—I've got to fly right by that Chilkat clear-cut! Now, I'm embarrassed. Every time I fly by there, somebody in the plane's always asking, 'Oh, what's that, what's going on down there?' I guess I'm getting pretty rabid," he says, surprised at his own frustrations and newfound concerns for the land. "Used to be the other way."

One Thanksgiving, a time when Lynn and his relatives return to their hometown of Haines, he decided to visit Chilkat eagle preserve, an area once slated for logging despite the fact that bald eagles mass here in huge numbers every November or December, drawn by mobs of chum salmon.

"So we fly over there, my brother and I," recalls Lynn. "There's 30 or 40 eagles in a single tree, a thousand eagles within eyeshot. And my brother says, 'Gee, were all these eagles here when *we* were kids?' "

Lynn laughs out loud. "Funny, you know? I mean, we never gave 'em a second thought when we lived there. It was just a bunch of eagles, no big deal. We didn't know what we *had*."

Nature's unsparing economies transform an ailing spruce into a convenient perch—whence this northern hawk-owl can swoop down on diverse victims.

FOLLOWING PAGES: Bleak terrain and scarce rations daunt predators, allowing placid mountain goats—adept and adapted—to thrive.

MICHAEL H. FRANCIS. FOLLOWING PAGES: TOM BEAN

*Still waters belie
disputes that run deep.
Tongass National Forest,
largest in the nation,
represents elusive
prosperity to Alaskan
loggers and mill workers.
Yet its old growth,
untouched since creation,
offers an ideal home to
Sitka black-tailed deer
(above) and hundreds of
other species—including
endangered bald eagles.*

"*W*e do have our wet times and our cold times, but even then there is a natural beauty that insists on manifesting itself," wrote an Alaskan journalist in 1960. Panhandle loveliness manifests itself not only in antique trees and soaring eagles, but also in humble bogs and boreal toads.

FOLLOWING PAGES: Wild raspberry leaves make a summer salad for a porcupine and her offspring. The abundant, varied vegetation of warmer months comes as a welcome change from monotonous winter bark. These quilled rodents can safely turn their backs on predators.

KENNAN WARD, GERRY ELLIS (OPPOSITE).
FOLLOWING PAGES: TOM AND PAT LEESON / DRK PHOTO

*G*lacier Bay is but two centuries old, formed by the fastest glacial retreat on record. Moss caressed raw hills, humpbacks (right) breached in teeming waters, spruce and hemlock took root—all punctuated by the "white thunder" of glacial calving (above).

FOLLOWING PAGES: Misty Fiords National Monument holds varied habitats: forest, muskeg, and meadow.

Snow geese in summer fill the sky above their tundra breeding grounds in Arctic National Wildlife Refuge; they winter far to the south.

FOLLOWING PAGES: Two of Denali's brown bears—usually called grizzlies in the Interior—forage for September blueberries among dwarf willows and birch.

Alaska *is* unique. Its land is enormous. Its wildlife communities—most of them—remain large and widespread. Extensive reserves already stand in place. The fact that this state has its own endangered species act, quite apart from federal statutes, says a lot about local attitudes toward wildlife.

Yet high-minded laws and huge reserves are only a beginning. John Schoen, a conservation biologist for Alaska's Department of Fish and Game, warns, "I don't think there's any place in the world where we can manage biological diversity purely on preserves. What's going on *outside* the boundaries may be every bit as important as what's going on inside."

Especially in Alaska, where wildlife issues are myriad, human population and developments are burgeoning, and special interests continually lobby and counterlobby for advantage. "We need," John adds, "to have a broader perspective, and we need to keep in mind the connections."

Perspective, connections—and hard choices. These are the tools needed to secure the future of Alaskan wildlife. Identify crucial wildlife corridors that link disparate areas, for example, and keep them intact. (Otherwise, populations may become fragmented, causing gene pools to lose the diversity that is nature's key to survival.) Aggregate development sites and transportation corridors, rather than scattering them piecemeal over the land.

Many people still say that hey, no worry, Alaska's big. There's room enough for all. But already, where caribou once wandered, semitrailers stream past, their mudflaps emblazoned "North to the Future."

"A single development may not be a problem in itself," John explains. "But it's a beachhead. You get a road and an industrial site, and that makes it more cost-efficient to have something else, and then something else. I'm not saying we should lock this country up. I'm saying that we need to be thinking way ahead of ourselves, 50 or 100 years into the future."

It's a belief widely shared by wildlife biologists throughout the state. Alaska's magnificent wildlife requires magnificent spaces; many species are nearly as sensitive to habitat fragmentation as they are to habitat loss, and while existing reserves are large, they also are politically fragmented.

"Every agency has its own habitat classification system," notes John, "and goes about business from its frame of reference, and there's not very effective coordination between them."

Cooperation is needed, now—and not just among bureaucrats, he adds. "Development interests are going to have to talk to conservation interests and natural resource managers in a much more positive, constructive way than they have in the past." So, too, will citizens throughout the nation. As Alaskans know only too well, the bulk of the Last Frontier is not state but federal land. Whether managed by the Forest Service or Fish and Wildlife or some other bureau, that land belongs to *all* Americans. Will it and its stunning collection of wildlife be managed wisely, so as to yield perpetual returns, or will it be squandered in the names of progress and expediency? Whatever Alaska does—or doesn't—become is up to all of us.

Seeking a mate, a bull moose pauses beside a nameless tundra pond in Denali National Park, where September sunlight brightens Mount Silverthrone.

MARK NEWMAN / EARTH IMAGES

AREA CLOSED

**CLOSED TO ALL ENTRY
CRITICAL WILDLIFE HABITAT**

Epilogue:
Last Chance, Best Hope